Another

𝖂𝖔𝖗𝖉 𝕶𝖊𝖞𝖘

book by

Duane Spencer

Word Keys Which Unlock Christmas

by

Duane Spencer

GRACE BIBLE PRESS
Box 13397
San Antonio, Texas 78213

Index

JESUS - - - - - - - - - - - - - - - - Page   1

CHRIST - - - - - - - - - - - - - - - Page 13

LORD - - - - - - - - - - - - - - - - Page 25

VIRGIN BIRTH - - - - - - - - - Page 37

VIRGIN MARY - - - - - - - - - - Page 49

WISE MEN - - - - - - - - - - - - Page 61

STAR - - - - - - - - - - - - - - - - - Page 73

SALVATION - - - - - - - - - - - - Page 85

Jesus

JESUS IS UNDOUBTEDLY the sweetest name in world to the ear of a born-again Believer. No other name has excited the adoration of as many millions, or inspired as many cheerful songs of worship and praise, as has "the Name which is above every other name" — the precious name of Jesus.

JOHN NEWTON expressed this so beautifully in one of his hymns when he wrote:

> How sweet the Name of Jesus sounds
> In a Believer's ear;
> It soothes his sorrows, heals his wounds,
> And drives away his fear.

One has only to turn to the index of his Christian hymnal to discover that nearly all of the hymns listed under "J" are built on the name of Jesus. Then, as his eye passes over the other divisions of the index, he observes that a great percentage of the titles are built around this precious name.

> Jesus! Oh how sweet the Name!
> Jesus! Every day the same!
> Jesus! Let all saints proclaim
> Its worthy praise forever!

No other religion in the world has the abundance of joyous songs as does the Christian faith. And, if the content of the songs be examined, it becomes quite evident that the source of inspiration is the blessed Second Person of the Holy Trinity, the Lord Jesus.

Frederick Whitfield, the 19th century hymn writer, has expressed the sentiments of all who are born of God when he sang:

> There is a Name I love to hear,
> I love to sing its worth;
> It sounds like music in mine ear,
> The sweetest name on earth!
>> Oh, how I love Jesus!
>> Oh, how I love Jesus!
>> Oh, how I love Jesus!
>> Because He first loved me!

"JESUS" WAS A POPULAR NAME

Many Christians are unaware of the fact that the name "Jesus" was a very popular Jewish name from the time that the Israelites settled in Palestine. This popularity lasted until around the second century A.D., when it disappeared from usage in the Jewish community, for quite obvious reasons. Three of the translators of the Septuagint version of the Old Testament, which is the translation of the Hebrew Bible into Greek, were men by the name of Jesus. At least 20 persons by the name of Jesus are mentioned by the Jewish historian Josephus. Of these, at least half were contemporaries of our Lord! In fact the New Testament itself gives two certain examples of Jewish men who bore the same name as our Lord. The one, a renegade Jew who had taken up sorcery in the island of Cyprus, is identified by the Jewish word for "son," the word "bar." The other, a fellow worker of the apostle Paul, is identified as belonging to the "circumcision," a derisive name given Jews by Gentiles. In Acts 13:6 we read that Paul and Barnabas found a "certain sorcerer, a false prophet, a Jew, whose name was Bar-jesus." Again, in Colossians 4:11, where the apostle Paul concludes his epistle with a word of greeting from the brethren with him we read of one named "Jesus, who is called Justus."

There are possibly other New Testament passages in which others bear the name Jesus, but the manuscripts vacillate as to the form. Matthew 27:16 is an example of this. Several of the ancient manuscripts call Barabbas, the malefactor released by Pilate during the trial of Jesus, by the name Jesus Barabbas. It is certainly understandable why the devout scribes who translated the New Testament Scriptures hesitated to give the full name of an evil man who was also named Jesus. However, we mention it in passing because we are seeking to show that the name of our Lord was quite common in the Jewish community.

"JESUS" THE SAME AS "JOSHUA"

We do not have to go far to discover why the name "Jesus" was so popular among the Jews. The fact of the matter is that "Jesus" is the Greek form of the Hebrew name "Joshua." This name had been borne by two illustrious individuals in former periods of Jewish history — Joshua, the great warrior who succeeded Moses in the command of Israel, and Jeshua, the high priest who served during the period following the return from the Babylonian captivity. In other words the name was popular with the Jews because two great heroes, one a military man and the other a priest, has made the name glorious in their eyes.

THE FORMING OF THE NAME

It is of further interest to note that these names, Jesus, Jeshua, and Joshua, which are simply the same name spelled in different ways, are a compound made up of two very important words. The one is the most holy of all of the names of God, and the other is a word which means "saving" or "salvation."

In the beginning, when Joshua was called to succeed Moses, his name was Hosea. This name, Hosea, is spelled in a variety of ways in the King James version of the Bible. In Numbers 13:16 it is spelled OSHEA. To this name, which means "salvation," Moses added the abbreviated Hebrew form for Jehovah, using it as a prefix, making the compound name JAH-HOSHUA, which (later) contracted to the more common form, Joshua.

If you will read Numbers 13:16 you will discover that "Moses called OSHEA, the son of Nun, JE-HOSHUA." Later on, in Numbers 14:38, in connection with the death report on the faithless spies, the name of the son of Nun is given simply as "Joshua."

There is also a record of a pre-exilic Joshua (or Jesus) in the genealogy of Mary recorded in Luke 3:

29. In Rabbinic literature it is found to be the name given the ninth priestly class.

"JOSHUA," A BANNER NAME

It is quite apparent that the alteration of the name of the son of Nun from HOSEA to JOSHUA was designed to communicate a message to the troops of Israel. Every time someone asked, "Who is your leader?" the answer would come. "Jehovah is Saviour!" for that is exactly what the name Joshua said! As great a military strategist as Joshua was, his name was never spoken without at the same time testifying that God was the real Power behind the victories. That was a day when the credit was not given to military leaders, but to Jehovah of Hosts, the Almightly Who is the real Deliverer (or Saviour) of His people!

Of course we know that God uses men, and Joshua the son of Nun was chosen of Jehovah as a human agent through whom He would lead Israel to victory over their physical enemies. No one knew this better than Jesus, the son of Nun. He knew Who the True Captain of the hosts of the LORD really was, and we read in Joshua 5:13-15 that he fell on his face and worshipped Him!

JOSHUA, A TYPE OF JESUS CHRIST

As we compare Scripture with Scripture it becomes apparent that the Joshua of the Old Testament, whose name can just as accurately be translated "Jesus," is actually a type or figure of our dear Lord in His role

as the Deliverer or Saviour of the people of God. It is
not only true that our Joshua will lead us in the Day
of Jehovah, against the enemies of God, but it is also
true that He gives us victory against the demonic
forces that seek to keep us from occupying until
Jesus comes. In his great passage in Ephesians 6 which
describes the "whole armor of God," the apostle Paul
declares that "we wrestle not against flesh and blood,
but against principalities, against powers, against the
rulers of the darkness of this world, against spiritual
wickedness in the heavenlies." (Eph. 6:12) These
terms, "principalities" and "powers," are titles for
angelic orders in the echelon of Satan's forces. Our
"Joshua," the Lord Jesus Christ, in Whom God Almightly is resident, is the One who leads us to victory
over our real enemies, the world, the flesh, and the
devil. (Cf. Revelation 19:11-16 and Hebrews 12:2.)

It is a wonderful thing to know, as we battle with
the demonic forces which are behind the world's way
of life, that "He who is in us is greater than he who is
in the world." In other words, Christ, Who indwells
the Believer, is greater than Satan whose dwelling is
the atmosphere about the earth. (Eph. 2:2 compared with I John 4:4).

The apostle Paul expresses the same truth in the
triumphant war cry of Romans 8:21—
      If God be for us
      Who can be against us!
As followers of the Eternal Son of God we have no
anxieties about the outcome of the cosmic conflict for
our Captain is Jesus Christ, the KING of kings!

JESHUA, A TYPE OF JESUS CHRIST

Just as Joshua (Jesus) the son of Nun is a type of Jesus Christ as the great Saviour (Deliverer) of the people of God, so Jeshua (Jesus) the son of Josedech is a type of Jesus Christ the great High Priest of God's elect. (Cf. Zechariah 3:1 with Hebrews 3:1).

In the vision of Zechariah 3 the high priest Jeshua appears in the court of Jehovah, clad in filthy garments, and under accusation of Satan. Now, in order to understand this vision, we must think like an oriental (for the Jew is an oriental). The passage focuses attention upon the garments worn by the high priest. We read — "Now Jeshua (Joshua) the high priest was clothed with filthy garments, and stood before the angel. And he answered and spoke unto those who stood before him, saying, Take away the filthy garments from him. And, unto him he said, Behold, I have caused thine uniquity to pass from thee, and I will clothe thee with a change of raiment. And I said, Let them set a clean turban upon his head. So they set upon his head a clean turban, and clothed him with garments."

It is clearly seen that the garments referred to here are used as an oriental symbol. Something is being said by the action taking place. This is affirmed by Zechariah 3:5, where the meaning of the change has been explained by the statement: "Behold, I have caused thine iniquity to pass from thee . . . "

As this passage is viewed in context it will be seen

that Jeshua (Joshua) the high priest stands in the vision as the Representative of Israel, the people of Jehovah. Strangely enough, it is he, and not a sacrificial lamb, that is seen bearing the guilt of Israel. This, of course, means that Jeshua stands as the substitute for the people of God, as well as their priest. He is under accusation of Satan for it is a law of God that the one upon whom the sins are laid must bear the punishment as well as the guilt and shame. (Cf. Isaiah 53:6 with John I:29.)

In the vision, therefore, the "filthy garments" are a symbol of sin. The purpose of the vision is to show the prophet (and us) that there is a High Priest who is actually the sin-bearer of the people of God, for the "LORD has laid on Him the iniquity of us all." He is both High Priest and Sacrifice. (Hebrews 9:11-12) Clad in the garments of our humanity our Jeshua was made to be sin for us, when he hung on the cross, but when He comes again He will be clad in a sin-free body, for Satan is rebuked and our High Priest stands in triumph as the Omnipotent, Omniscient, resurrected Sacrificial Victim who is KING as well as Priest!

HOSEA, A TYPE OF JESUS CHRIST

Just as Joshua the son of Nun is a type of Christ as our King-Deliverer, and Jeshua the son of Josedech is type of Christ as our Priest-Sacrifice, so the prophet Hosea is a type of Christ as Prophet-Redeemer.

We have previously noted that the name Joshua was made by taking the name Hosea (Oshea) and prefixing the Divine Title, JAH, which is an abbreviation of Yahweh or Jehovah. This combination made a banner name which declared that "Jehovah is Salvation" to all of the troops under Joshua, as well as to their enemies. When this name was given to the son of Mary, by God through His messenger, it was purposing to proclaim to His people and His enemies that Jesus is He who delivers from sin and Satan. (Cf. Matthew 1: 21.)

Careful students of the Word of God, who have understood Semitic symbolism, have long realized that the person and work of our Saviour is prophetically expressed in the roles played by the Old Testament personages bearing His holy Name in one form or another. The prophet Hosea, or Hoshea as it is properly pronounced, is no exception.

Marvin Vincent (in his *Word Studies in the New Testament)* states the case, observing that it is no mere fancy which sees a suggestion and a foreshadowing of the PROPHETIC work of Jesus in the ministry of Hosea. (Cf. Romans 9:25). "He is, in a peculiar sense, the prophet of grace and salvation, placing his hope in God's personal coming as the refuge and strength of humanity; in the purification of human life by its contact with the divine. The great truth which he has to teach is the love of Jehovah to Israel as expressed in the relation of HUSBAND, an idea which pervades his prophecy, and which is generated by his own sad domestic experience. He foreshadows Jesus in his pointed warnings against sin, his repeated offers of divine mercy, and his patient, forbearing love, as manifested in his dealing with an unfaithful and dissolute wife, whose soul he succeeded in rescuing from sin and death (Hosea i. - iii.). So long as he lived he was one continual, living prophecy of the tenderness of God toward sinners; a picture of God's love for us when alien from Him, and with nothing in us to love."

If you have not read the remarkable story of the prophet Hosea and his "wife of whoredoms," you ought to do so at your earliest opportunity. Briefly, the story tells how the Word of Jehovah came to the prophet and commanded him to take a whore for a wife as a dramatic portrayal of the fact that Jehovah knowingly took Israel to be his spiritual "wife" even though He foreknew her infidelity. Hence the purchase of Hosea's unfaithful wife from the slave block, by the prophet, speaks of God our Saviour who has redeemed us from slavery to sin.

"JESUS" IN THE GOSPELS

In the Gospel accounts of the Person and Work of our Lord, the name "Jesus" particularly stresses His humanity. It is by this name that He is addressed, and discussed among the people of Israel. Since there were many rabbis by the same name they distinguished our Lord by adding such phrases as "from Nazareth of Galilee," or "the Nazarene." He is also called "son of David" by the people, identifying Him as a descendant of the great Hebrew warrior-king. The multitude, in Matthew 21:11, answers the question, "Who is this? by saying, "This is Jesus the prophet of Nazareth of Galilee."

It is by the name "Jesus" that the Son of God revealed Himself to Saul of Tarsus, and it is by this dear name that He is referred to by the angels at the time of His ascension into heaven. When the heavens are opened to Stephen, at the time of his martyrdom, he sees Jesus at the right hand of Jehovah.

Since Jesus is the God-Man Who is both True God and True Man, the name associated with His humanity is inevitably associated with the divine title "Lord" or the Greek name of Messiah, "the Christ." Whenever the apostle Paul uses the simple title of "Jesus" in his epistles, he inevitably is stressing His humanity. (Over half of these instances occur in I Thessalonians 4:14 and II Corinthians 4:11-14.) Whenever he uses the compounds, "Jesus Christ," or "Lord Jesus," the emphasis is invariably upon the fact that our Saviour is both God and Man.

It was his firm faith in the testimony of Scripture that Jesus Christ is God Incarnate, (that is, Jehovah manifested in human form in the midst of mankind) that caused the great poet Charles Wesley to sing:

> Christ by highest heaven adored;
> Christ, the Everlasting Lord!
> Late in time behold Him come,
> Offspring of the virgin's womb:
> Veiled in flesh the Godhead see!
> Hail, Incarnate Deity!
> Pleased as man with men to dwell,
> Jesus, our Emmanuel!
> Hark! The herald angels sing,
> "Glory to the newborn King!"

It is not without reason that Paul insists to Titus that Jesus is "that great God and our Saviour." If he is not God, then He is not Saviour from sin and its penalty! The critics of Jesus were absolutely right when they declared that "only God can forgive sin." Their blasphemy lay in the fact that they refused to believe Him to be Whom He declared Himself to be, by both word and work — Jehovah God in the flesh.

Peter in his great address to the Sanhedrin, as recorded in the fourth chapter of Acts, states plainly:

"There is no other name under heaven,
given among men, whereby we must be saved."

Surely Christmas is a time when we ought to have our thoughts centered in Him for whom the season was named — the dear Lord Jesus. Rather than preoccupation with earthly gifts which soon are relegated to the trash heap, let us seek after the Giver of every good and perfect gift which never fades away—gifts which are garrisoned in heaven for us who trust in Jesus.

Let our joy be in Him whose very name declares that He is Jehovah our Salvation. Let the season of Christmas be one in which we Believers offer Him to a lost and dying world as Saviour and Lord.

Joy to the world! The LORD is come!
Let earth receive her king!
Let every heart prepare Him room,
And heaven and nature sing!

Christ

ONE OF THE TITLES of our blessed Lord is "Christ." Our English word "Christ" is the transliteration of the Greek verbal adjective CHRISTOS, just as its synonym "Messiah" is derived from the Hebrew participle MASHIACH. Both words mean "anointed" Therefore, to say that Jesus is The Christ is to declare that He is the Lord's Anointed One.

As the Bible student reads the Gospel accounts he is struck by the fact that our Lord is usually referred to as "Jesus," as we have seen in a previous study of that key Bible word. However, in our study of the epistles, we discover that He is more often referred to as "Christ." This is quite understandable since the gospels deal with the time of His humiliation, while the epistles lift Him up as the exalted One.

In Peter's sermon on the Day of Pentecost the apostle states the issue plainly to the Jews, saying:

"Therefore, let all the House of Israel know assuredly that God has made that same Jesus, whom ye have crucified, both Lord and CHRIST." (Acts 2:36)

As we shall see in this word study, Jesus is declared to be the Messiah of the Jew in unmistakable terms. Before His resurrection our Lord was spoken of as "the Christ" to establish His identity in the minds of the people. After His resurrection, however, when the recognition of Jesus as the Messiah had become more general, the term is often used without the definite article. In such instances it becomes a compound title, "Jesus Christ," to which the further identifying appellation "Lord" is often added.

There can absolutely be no doubt but that the early church firmly believed and taught that Jesus of Nazareth is the Messiah of the Jew, the Christ of God for whom Israel had wept down through the centuries. The New Testament is simply loaded with witnesses which agree that Jesus is the Christ.

THE WITNESSES AGREE!

ANDREW, a disciple of John the baptizer, who heard the Way Preparer identify Jesus as the "Lamb of God who takes away the sin of the world," taught that our Lord is the Messiah of the Jew. It will be remembered that he left John and followed Jesus, when he heard that amazing identification. (Cf. Genesis 22:8 with John 1:29) After a period of wonderful fellowship and discussion with the Master, Andrew rushed out to find his brother Simon, saying:

"We have found the Christ!" (Jn. 1:41)

SIMON, later named Peter, became equally convinced that Jesus is the Messiah of Israel and that Andrew's testimony was true. On the occasion that our Lord was probing the spiritual consciousness of His disciples at Ceasarea Philippi, about twenty five miles to the north of the Sea of Galilee, Peter gave his great testament of faith. When Jesus said, "Whom do you all say that I am ?"Peter leaped to his feet and cried:

> "You are the Christ!
> You are the Son of the Living God!"
> (Matthew 16:16)

MARK, in the very first verse of his earliest of the gospel accounts, writes that Jesus is the CHRIST, the Son of the Living God.

The witnesses agree! Jesus IS the Christ!

JOHN, the Beloved Disciple who was so close to the heart of our Lord, declares that his entire Gospel is written with one purpose in mind, namely to show that Jesus is Israel's Messiah. In the closing verses of the twentieth chapter of the Gospel bearing his name, John writes:

> "Many other signs truly did Jesus in the presence of His disciples, which are not written in this book; but these are written that ye might believe that Jesus is the Christ, the Son of God; and that believing ye might have Life through His Name!"
> (John 20:30-31)

THE WITNESSES AGREE!

MARTHA, the older sister of Mary and Lazarus of Bethany, believed that Jesus is the Messiah of Israel. It is her emphatic declaration in John 11:27:

"I believe you to be the Christ, the Son of God."

PETER, in his sermon on the Day of Pentecost, as we have already noted, preached Jesus as the CHRIST, as well as Lord.

PAUL, testifying before the Jews of the synogogue of Damacus, insisted that Jesus is The Christ.

THE LORD JESUS, Himself. knew that He was the promised Messiah, the Christ of Israel. Not only did He take unto Himself such Messianic titles as "Son of Man." but He accepted the testimony that He is indeed "the Holy One of God." He openly declares to the woman at the well of Sychar. and to the high priest at His trial. that He is "the Christ." (Cf. John 4:25-26 with Matthew 26:63-64.)

THE WRITER OF HEBREWS, referring to the Messianic Psalm 110:4. declares that Jesus is the Eternal King-Priest of the Melchizidekian order. which is to say that He must indeed be The Messiah of Israel!

Each of the witnesses has borne his or her testimony on the basis of the Old Testament prophecies or references to the Messiah of Israel the LORD'S Anointed One.

MESSIAH, THE SON OF MAN

Our Lord had a definite predeliction for the Messianic title, "Son of Man." He scrupulously avoided the appellation ' Messiah." but, with equal care, He made use of the designation, "Son of Man." When the apostle Peter confessed Jesus to be "the Messiah" at Caesarea Philippi, in response to our Saviour's question, "Whom say ye that I am? " Jesus replied that "the Son of Man must suffer many things." (Mark 8:29 ff.) Again, when the high priest interrogated Him, saying. 'Are you the Messiah. the Son of the Blessed? " Jesus responded by identifying Himself as the Cloud Man as the rabbis called the Son of Man in Daniel 7:13.

MESSIAH. "HE WHO COMETH"

The One who comes in the clouds is, of course, the Christ of the Second Advent. He is, nevertheless, "this same Jesus" who ascended into heaven in the cloud of the glory. It must be remembered that it can also be said "Now is the last day" (I John 2:18) for the Parousia of Christ will being to completion that which was initiated concerning the "last things" at His first advent. There can be no doubt but that Messiah is the "Blessed One" who comes in the name of Jehovah in Psalm 118:26. Later, as we study the words "name" and "blessed" we shall discover that much is contained in this seemingly simple phrase! The One who is coming in the clouds of the glory is the Son of Man who is none other than the Christ of God.

Even the strange title "Ebed Jeveh," or ' Servant of Jehovah," has Messianic overtones. It was because Jesus so plainly identified Himself with the Suffering Servant of Isaiah 53 that the leaders of Israel rejected Him as the Christ. This concept of Messiah was so alien to the popular ideas of His time, in which Christ was depicted only in His role as a military deliverer, one who would break the bonds of the oppressor, that His evident role as Ebed Javeh was totally repugnant. Yet it may be safely stated that the teaching of Jesus and the early church concerning His Messiahship can not be truly understood apart from Isaiah 53. This is particularly true with regards such passages as Phil. 2:7-9 where Paul speaks of Him who took the "form of a servant" and was obedient unto death.

FOUR "CHRIST" CATEGORIES

We must always remember the law of the common from the particular, with regards biblical titles. For example. many are called "sons of God" because the Lord Jesus is the unique Son of God. The many are referred to as "rocks" (plural), for the simple reason that God the Son is THE Rock, singular. Paul is a "servant of God" because Jesus Christ is THE Servant of God. The common or plural derive their titles from the Unique One. Without the Son of God there would be no "sons of God," plural, Without Jesus as THE Christ of God there would be no "christs of God," plural. It is the reality of the Particular which causes to be the common or many. Keep this in mind as we speak of the four categories of "anointed ones" in the Old Testament.

In the Old Testament there are four categories of persons who bore the general title of "christ" or the "anointed one." These were the prophets. priests, kings, and the chosen people of God.

THE PROPHETS of God were anointed for office. Elisha, for example, was anointed to succeed Elijah as spokesman for Jehovah. (I Kings 19:16) As such he, as well as all of the other prophets, were spoken of as "anointed ones of God" which is the equivalent of saying that they were "christs of God."

THE PRIESTS of God were also anointed for office. The high priest, in particular, as a "son of Aaron," was anointed by the puring of oil over his head. The oil of anointing was also sprinkled upon his garments and upon the furniture of the tabernacle. (Exodus 29)

THE KINGS of Israel were anointed before being inducted to rule. You will remember that David referred to King Saul as "the LORD's anointed." Samuel, at the time he anointed King Saul, kissed him and said: "Has not the LORD anointed you to be prince over His people Israel?" (Cf. I Samuel 24:10, 10:1; 16:13; and I Kings 1:39.)

THE CHOSEN PEOPLE of God are also spoken of as the LORD's "anointed," which is to say, "Jehovah's Christs" or "Jehovah's Messiahs". An example of this is to be seen in the poetic parallelism of Habakkuk—

> "Thou didst go forth
> for the salvation of Thy people,
> for the salvation of Thine anointed." (3:13)

The student of Hebrew poetry knows that the writer is here declaring that the going forth of Jehovah on behalf of His people to deliver them was saving action on behalf of his "anointed ones" or "christs." Therefor the people of God, as well as the prophets, priests, and kings of God, are considered to be the LORD's Christs. Martin Luther recognized this when he said to his people that they must remember that they were "little christs."

Other passages which speak of the people of God as His "anointed (ones)" are scattered throughout the Psalms of David. Take Psalm 28:8-9 for example:

> "The LORD is their strength,
> He is the saving strength of the anointed."

Here it is declared that Jehovah is the strength of His people, for it is the people to whom the "their" refers. Then, in the parallel line, they are identified as "the anointed." (Cf. Psalm 84:9; 89:38, 51)

JESUS IS "THE PROPHET"

Jesus completely fulfills the prophecy of Deuteronomy 18:18 according to Peter in Acts 3:22. Having identified Jesus as the Messiah (or Christ) of Israel, the apostles cries out:

"Moses truly said to the fathers, the LORD your God shall raise up a prophet of your brethren like unto me. Him shall you hear in all things that He shall say unto you. And it shall come to pass that every soul that will not hear The Prophet shall be destroyed from among My People." (Acts 3:22)

The prophet of the Old Testament was a man who spoke for Jehovah as a chosen and annointed mouthpiece of God. Jesus is "THE PROPHET" of Jehovah for He speaks as God for God, and not as mere man speaking for God. As the divine Logos of God who is none other than God the Son Himself, Jesus constantly affirmed that He spoke for God as God's apostle.

"I do not speak of My own authority. My Father Who has sent Me has instructed Me as to what I shall say, and what I am to proclaim. I know that His commandment is Life Eternal. Therefore I say only what He has instructed Me to say."
(Jn. 12:49-50)

It is to be further observed that "The Prophet" of whom Moses spoke, and whom Peter identified as The Christ of God, was to be received or else! (The Hebrew word "hear" means to accept and to act.)

Therefore, when the Great Lawgiver declares, "And it shall come to pass that every soul that will not hear The Prophet shall be destroyed from among My people." It is for this reason that we find that acceptance of the Word of Jesus is a life and death matter."

> "He who believes on the Son has everlasting Life; and he who believes not the Son shall not see Life, but the wrath of God abideth on him." (John 3:36)

THE WITNESSES AGREE . . . Jesus is the Christ!

JESUS IS "THE PRIEST"

It was well-known to the Jews that their Messiah was an eternal Priest. David, the sweet singer of Israel, declared the immutable covenant of Jehovah with Messiah by the oath:

> "Thou art a priest forever
> after the order of Melchizedek."

The historical reference is to the mysterious King of Peace and Righteousness before Whom Abram worshipped and unto Whom he presented his tithe. (See Genesis 14:17-22) The New Testament writer to the Hebrews carefully identifies the Lord Jesus with this Melchizedek and His Divine Order, declaring Christ to be the High Priest of the Most High God. (Cf. Hebrews 7) He says specifically in Hebrews 3:1—

> Jesus is "The Apostle" (spokesman for God)
> Jesus is "High Priest" (spokesman for man)
> Jesus is the "Christ" (The LORD's Annointed)

THE WITNESSES AGREE . . . Jesus is The Christ!

Perhaps here we should observe something that we also speak about in detail in our study of the word Mediator. The role of the prophet or apostle is to speak for God to man. The role of the high priest is to speak for man to God. (Observe that the 'direction' of these two roles is opposite.) Jesus is the Christ-prophet of God because He speaks as God for God, and He is the Christ-priest because He speaks as Man for man. This perfect representation of both parties — God and man — thereby makes Jesus to be the true Mediator.

JESUS IS "THE KING"

Not only is Jesus the Christ because He is the complete fulfilment of all that the office of the annointed prophets declared; and the Christ because He is the absolute fulfilment of all that the office of the annointed priests declared; but He is the triumphant fulfilment of all that the anointed kings of Israel symbolically declared.

In the book of Revelation where Jesus is so remarkably unveiled as the Eternal God, our Lord is said to be "King of kings and Lord of lords." (19:16) He is not to be considered simply one among many potentates, but as the Absolute Power Who is Sovereign Ruler over all other powers, whether human or angelic. It is the "One Who cometh" in the name of the Blessed (that is in the name of Jehovah), and in the clouds of heaven, who is The Christ. Jesus is that One. He is the King-Priest of Zechariah 6:13 and Hebrews seven. He is the Priestly Monarch who stands in the midst of the Church in the Son of Man Vision of Revelation 1:13. It is He for Whom the Chruch looks to come from heaven to cast down God's enemies.

THE WITNESSES AGREE . . . Jesus is the Christ!

We have said that the people of God, in the Old Testament, are also considered to be the Lord's annointed (ie., the Lord's "christs.") This, again, like the roles of prophet, priest, and king, is a foreshadowing of Christ Jesus. In the New Testament the people of God who are His "anointed ones" are seen to be the Body of Christ which is the Church. Paul in II Corinthians 1:21-22 states specifically:

"Now He who establishes us with you in
CHRIST, and has ANOINTED us, is God,
Who has also sealed us, and hath given us
the earnest of the Spirit in our hearts."

During the Church Age all believers are "anointed" of God by the Holy Spirit. Just as the Levitical priests were anointed with oil, upon induction into the priesthood, so the Believer is anointed with the Holy Spirit upon his induction into the kingly priesthood through the new birth. (Cf. I Peter 2:9)

It is the sheep of the Lord whose heads are said to be "anointed with oil" in the 23rd Psalm, and we are "the sheep of His pasture." When He stood in the little synagogue of Nazareth to read from the Isaiah scroll, Jesus insisted that He was the Anointed One of whom the prophet spoke. It is He who is anointed with the "oil of gladness" above all others (Hebrews 1:9) for He is the Christ child hated by the kings of the earth. (Acts 4:27) Just as God anointed His unique Son, Jesus, declaring Him to be   Israel's

Messiah (Acts 10:38), so, also, the born-again Believer has the "unction" or "anointing of the Spirit of God.

THE WITNESSES AGREE . . . Jesus is the CHRIST! (And, praise God, every born-again Believer is also "anointed of God" by the Holy Spirit! Hallelujah!

> Hark! the herald angels sing
> "Glory to the newborn king:
> Peace on earth, and mercy mild,
> God and sinners reconciled!"
> Joyful, all ye nations, rise,
> Join the triumph of the skies;
> With th'angelic hosts proclaim,
> "Christ is born in Bethlehem!"
> Hark! the herald angels sing
> "Glory to the newborn King!"

> Christ, O Christ to Thee we sing,
> Born as Prophet, Priest and King;
> We as "little christs" on earth,
> Now extol Thy wondrous birth!
> Thou Who laid His glory by,
> Born that man no more may die,
> Born to raise Thy sons from earth,
> Born to give us Second Birth!
> Hark! the herald angels sing,
> "Glory to the newborn King!"

Lord

THE TITLE "LORD" is undoubtedly one of the most important honorific titles of Jesus Christ in the New Testament because it inevitably leads to His identification as the blessed Second Person of the Godhead. He is identified as the Incarnate God in many other ways in Scripture, but no other title is more exalted than "Lord" in proclaiming His Deity and His equality with God the Father.

TWO TERMS TRANSLATED "LORD"

In the New Testament there are two meaningful terms rendered by the English word "Lord" by the translators. The more common of the two is KURIOS (koo-ree-oss), and the other is DESPOTES (dess-paw-tace) from which our English word "despot" is derived. In the Scriptures both terms are used for Jesus as well as Jehovah and, in secular writings, for pagan dieties and for Emperors who were counted to be absolute masters and gods to be worshipped.

OUR LORD AS "DESPOT"

The term 'despotes' was used by the Greeks to describe certain gods or persons who exercised unrestricted power and absolute domination over others without any limitations or restraints whatsoever. It was particularly a term used of one who owned slaves and exercised the right to determine the disposal of their bodies as well as their abilities and energies.

Despotes is used with extreme care in the New Testament for the lord and owner of a house, for the master of slaves, and as a vocative in prayer to God. (I Timothy 6:1; II Timothy 2:21; Titus 2:9 and I Peter 2:18)

It is not at all surprising to find such an honorific title which insists upon absolute. unrestricted ownership and right of disposal of others, used for Jesus Christ and God the Father. Paul, in his epistles, does not hesitate for a moment to count himself as well as all Christians to be the "slaves of God." Furthermore he insists that we are "bought with a price." and that purchase price is the blood of Jesus Christ. (Cf. Acts 20:28) This concept of absolute ownership of the Believer by his Lord is inherent in the term "redeemed," for redemption speaks of the purchase of slaves from the market.

Trench comments that the term 'despotes' did "no doubt express on the lips of the faithful who used it, their sense of God's absolute disposal of His creatures, of His autocratic power, "who doeth according to His will in the army of heaven and among the ininhabitants of the earth" (Daniel 4:35). It is a term that implies, on the part of the user, a total prostration of self before the almightyness of God.

OUR LORD AS "KURIOS"

Some of the later Greek grammarians distinguished

between the terms 'despotes' and 'kurios' by saying that a man was 'despotes' in respect of his slaves and 'kurios' in regard to his wife and children. Peter in his first epistle, makes use of 'kurios' when he says that Sarah "obeyed Abraham, calling him lord." (3:6) There is, in this latter term, an implication of limitations, perhaps moral, or even self-imposed, but limitations nevertheless. There is also the underlying idea which insists that he who is 'kurios' will exercise his authority in consideration of the good of those over whom he wields it.

"LORDS MANY AND GODS MANY"

At the time the New Testament was being written there were "lords many and gods many." (I Cor. 8:5) In fact the terms 'theoi' (gods) and 'kurioi' (lords) kept such close company that they appear to be almost synonymous in their usage in the Greek writings. Not only are the pagan deities referred to as 'kurioi' in the papyri, but Eastern rulers and Roman Caesars as well. It was just at this very point that a terrible crisis was precipitated for the early followers of The Way. Demands were made by the State that the ruler be spoken of as "Lord" and worshipped as a god. The born-again Christian, like Paul, would reply that "there is but one God, the Father, of whom are the all things, and we in Him; and one Lord (Jesus Christ), by whom exist the all things, and we by Him." (I Corinthians 8:5-6) Such a response would be taken as a challenge to the lordship and godhood of the Roman Caesar, and such it was. The entire book of the Revelation of Jesus Christ serves as a polemic in oriental symbols which declare that Jesus Christ, and not Caesar, is 'kurios' and 'theos,' Lord and God.

The Lord Jesus, Himself, undoubtedly referred to the deification of the emperors when He said: "The kings of the Gentiles exercise LORDship over them." He, too, registered His protest against the worship of rulers as gods when He told the Herodians: "Render therefore to Caesar the things that are Caesar's, and to God the things that are God's." Since the State owns the coinage it issues it has a right to demand the payment of taxes in its own coinage. Since God is absolute Owner of all things as Creator and Redeemer it also stands to reason that He, too, expects a return on His "issue." The Kingdom of Christ may not be of this world, but it is, nevertheless, a kingdom in all reality, and the King is absolute owner of all in His domain.

JESUS CHRIST VERSUS CAESAR

It is difficult for many Christians to realize in this day and age why a simple term, such as "Lord," should precipitate a life-or-death crisis for the early Church. This is occasioned partially by the fact that the early followers of Jesus knew more basic Bible doctrine, and took what they knew more seriously, than do most Christians today. The other reason is that they knew what the term "Lord" meant.

Let me approach the explanation of their problem by sketching the historical background which created it, as far as the State was concerned. The Roman Empire spread like a giant octopus from the British Isles to the rim of the even greater Persian Empire. The problem of the Roman Senate was how to unify their vast conglomeration of city-states, nations, and tribes with their many languages and religions. It was obvious that a religion common to all must be found if real unity of spirit was to be achieved. None of the religions of the Western World was adaptable for this purpose, so a new religion had to be created for the sake of political unity. Since a great portion of the empire had been gained from kings who had deliberately willed their kingdoms to Rome, recognizing the great benefits that such a union would bring to the citizens of their nation, it was determined that a god should be created who would stand for all that the Pax Romana meant to the provincials.

You may not be aware of the fact that most of the provincials under the rule of Rome were grateful for their lot. They remembered the days when life was a perilous business, and they were more than thankful for the Pax Romana or Roman peace. Goodspeed, recognizing this fact, writes: "The provincial under Roman sway found himself in a position to conduct his business, provide for his family, send his letters, and make his journeys in security, thanks to the strong hand of Rome." As the peoples of the Empire recalled capricious tyrants of the past, contrasting their former insecure existence with their then present life under the impartial, though strict, justice of Rome, they were more than willing to worship the man who exemplified the Pax Romana. That man was

Caesar. Although some of the early Roman emperors hesitated to accept deification, the popular will of the people erected temples throughout the land, and his worship as a god began. Soon the will of the people became a decree of the Senate, and the emperor was declared to be both 'kurios' and 'theos', Lord and God.

When the powers of Rome saw the potential such veneration held, in terms of bringing political unity, they seized upon the idea of tying Caesar worship in with a loyalty oath. Therefore it was decreed that every citizen should burn incense to the god Caesar as an act of compulsory worship. This was done for only one reason; to test political loyalty to Rome. It had absolutely no purpose as a test of religious loyalty, for, as far as Rome was concerned, a man could worship as many gods as he wanted to just as long as he showed his loyalty to Rome by worshipping Caesar. All a man had to do, therefore, was burn a pinch of incense and say, "Caesar is Lord," and he would be given a Certificate of Loyalty. If he refused he would be branded a dangerous and disaffected citizen, and his life would be in danger from that moment on. Of course the Christian who believed, as did Paul, that "there is but one God, the Father, of whom are the all things, and we in Him; and one Lord (Jesus Christ), by whom exist the all things, and we by Him" would never say (even under penalty of death) "Caesar is Lord." As a result many, such as Polycarp the disciple of the apostle John, chose death rather than to use the terms 'kurios' or 'despotes' for other than the blessed Persons of the Holy Trinity.

"KING OF KINGS AND LORD OF LORDS"

When Jesus Christ, the Conquering General, comes in power and great glory to cast down the enemies of God at His parousia, He will come as King over all kings and Lord (kurios) over all lords. This is to say that His Second Coming will be as the One who is the absolute Owner and Sovereign over all created beings. To acknowledge Jesus Christ to be "Lord" is to declare that He is Jehovah manifest in the flesh.

We must recognize that the theology of the New Testament presupposes the Godhood of Jesus Christ. If it did not He would never have been allowed the title of kurios, Lord. This is really amazing when we realize that the human authors of the New Testament, for the most part, were monotheistic Jews. Yet it is strikingly apparent that they were firmly convinced that Jesus Christ is Immanuel, "God with us," for they transferred to Him, without hesitation, all that the Old Testament says about Jehovah! This indicates that they had pursued to its final outcome the doctrine of the Lordship of the Son of God, Jesus Christ.

THE WITNESS OF THE OLD TESTAMENT

I have just stated that the monotheistic authors of the New Testament transferred to Jesus all that the Old Testament says about Jehovah. Let me back that up with Scripture. The examples are many, but let me list just a few.

MARK 1:3 AND ISAIAH 40:3

Let us compare Mark 1:3, where Isaiah 40:3 is quoted, to see what I mean. In the Gospel we read: "The voice of one crying in the wilderness. 'Prepare ye the way of the Lord, make his paths straight." Here, in Mark, the word "Lord" translates the Greek word 'kurios,' the honorific title used for Jesus. The "way preparer" here is obviously John the Baptizer, and the "Lord" for whom the way is being prepared is plainly our Saviour. Now, turn to Isaiah 40:3, and you will see that in that passage the word LORD is spelled with all capital letters. This is the printer's way of telling you that the original Hebrew text has the word for "Jehovah." Since Jesus is declared to be the One called "LORD" by Isaiah it is quite clear that He is Jehovah as far as Mark is concerned!

ROMANS 10:13 AND JOEL 2:32

A most remarkable confirmation of our statement that the writers of the New Testament transferred to Jesus all that the Old Testament says about Jehovah is to be seen by contrasting Romans 10:13 with Joel 2:32. Paul says, "Whosoever shall call upon the name of the Lord (kurios) shall be saved." This is a direct quotation of the Jewish prophet, Joel, by Paul, a monotheistic Jew. Here, again, as you examine the text of the Old Testament prophet, you will discover that the word rendered 'kurios' by Paul is the Hebrew word JEHOVAH.

Since Paul applies this verse to Jesus, using 'kurios'

to render Jehovah, it is clear that he is declaring our Lord to be none other than God.

Not only are there numerous instances where the name "Jehovah" is transferred to Jesus, but the apostle Paul also affirms that to call Jesus 'kurios,' the honorific title used to translate the ineffable Name of Jehovah, is to glorify the heavenly Father! In Philippians two, verses nine through eleven, we read:

> "Wherefore God hath highly exalted Him, given Him a Name which is above every name that at the name of Jesus every knee should bow, of things in heaven, and things on earth, and things in the underworld; and that every tongue should confess that Jesus Christ is LORD (kurios), to the glory of God the Father."

For the monotheistic Jew the most exalted Name, bar none, was Jehovah. It was before this Name that all the peoples of the earth were to bow. It is this very Name of names that is transferred by Paul to Jesus, for Jesus is the heavenly Throne Sitter with the Father before whom all creatures must prostrate themselves in humble adoration.

Now it becomes more apparent why the early Church refused to say "Caesar is kurios" at the times of enrollment, even though they knew that it was simply a loyalty oath. Every indoctrinated Believer knew that 'kurios' was a title for a god, and he refused to call anyone other than the True God by the title "Lord."

Undoubtedly the Apostle Paul had Isaiah 45:22-23 in mind when he wrote to the Philippians that Jesus

Christ is LORD, and that every knee would one day bow before our Saviour. Isaiah quotes God as saying:

> "Look unto Me and be ye saved, all the ends of the earth! I am God, and there is none other! I have sworn by Myself, the Word is gone out of My mouth in righteousness, and shall not return, that unto Me every knee shall bow, and every tongue shall swear."

In this great passage the Speaker is Elohim, the God Who created the heavens and the earth. He declares that all of creation shall bow the knee before His divine majesty. Then, in verse 21 of the same passage, it will be noted that there is no other Saviour than the Sovereign God of heaven and earth. Therefore, when Paul declares Jesus to be Saviour and Lord before whom every knee shall bow, he is openly transferring the prerogatives and position of Deity to Him.

"THE ROCK" IS KURIOS

Oriental symbolism is used profusely throughout the Old Testament to describe both the Creator and the creature. One of these symbols is "rock." In his glorious song in Deuteronomy 32, Moses sings of the LORD (Jehovah) as the Rock of Israel. (32:4) He declares that God is the Rock of Salvation (v. 15) and the One who "begat" Israel. (v. 18) When Paul writes to the Corinthians he picks up this title for Jehovah from the books of Moses, and the Psalms of David, and declares that the "spiritual Rock" who led the children of Israel through the Red Sea was none other than the Lord Jesus Christ! (I Corinthians 10:4) Jesus Himself makes use of this same oriental symbol for Jehovah when He tells the disciples that upon "The Rock" He will build the True Church. Every Jew who heard Him thus speak knew that He was speaking of the LORD of Israel, the God of Jacob. (I Cor. 3:11 & Matthew 16:18)

No matter where one looks in the New Testament he finds Jesus described as Lord. This is especially true in the epistles where our dear Saviour is called 'kurios' nearly 150 times, and "Lord Jesus" nearly one hundred times more! It must be understood that this constant application of the term 'kurios' to Jesus must not be imagined as merely a formal mark of respect. It is the definite ascription to Him of universal absolute dominion not only over men, but over the whole universe of created beings. (Cf. Rom. 10:12)

POLYCARP AND THE TITLE "LORD"

One of the great historical examples of the willingness of Christians to die rather than to call anyone other than Jesus by the honorific 'Lord' is seen in the martyrdom of Polycarp, disciple of John the Beloved. The aged Bishop of Smyrna in Asia Minor was given the choice, "Worship Caesar as kurios, or die!" and he gave his immortal answer: "For eighty six years I have served Christ my Lord, and He has never done me wrong. How can I blaspheme my King who saved me? Light your faggots! I fear not the fire which burns for a season and after a while is quenched! Come! Do your will! Why do you delay?"

Not only is the Deity of Christ declared by calling Him 'kurios' (Lord), and by applying to Him many of the O.T. Scriptures which identify Him as Jehovah, but He is openly called God as well as Lord. We have already seen that these two terms 'kurios' and 'theos' (Lord and God) kept such close company in Greek that they were almost synonymous. This was not true in the secular koine Greek, but is seen constantly throughout the N.T. as well.

One of the most stirring examples of this is to be seen where Thomas, his doubts of the bodily resurrection removed, greets Jesus with the great cry: "My Lord and my God!" Yes, the witnesses agree, "Jesus is Lord" which is to say that Jesus is God!

Virgin Birth

THE DOCTRINE of the Virgin Birth is taught plainly in Scripture, and, as Bible doctrine, is to be believed just as heartily as any other doctrine. It is a vital doctrine concerning the Person of our Lord, and may not be dismissed with a "take it or leave it" kind of attitude. It is a 'must' for true Believers.

THE WITNESS OF THE EARLY CHURCH

There can be no doubt but that the Doctrine of the Virgin Birth was fully accepted throughout the primitive Church. Even in the second century, when so many extra-Biblical writings began to circulate, this basic doctrine was firmly believed and taught. For example: the early church father, Irenaeus, the pupil of Polycarp who was the disciple of the Apostle John, the beloved young friend of Jesus, treats the doctrine of the virgin birth of our Lord as fact. Other famous Bible teachers of the early church, such as Clement of Alexandria (Egypt), and Tertullian of North Africa discuss and teach it as fact (not as a 'myth' like the anti-Christs of our day). In fact there is such a re-remarkable concensus among all of the early Christian writers, as they defend the Faith against heretics, that there can be no doubt that the Doctrine of the Virgin Birth was widely accepted by the Church as a whole by the year AD 150.

THE TESTIMONY OF THE CREEDS

One of the earliest testimonies to the widespread belief of the early Christians in the fact of the virgin birth of Christ, is the Apostles' Creed. This testament of faith was produced in Gaul previous to the sixth century, and was built upon an old Roman baptismal confession. The Roman Creed, which also affirmed the faith of the Church in the virgin birth, is dated by even the most critical scholars to be at least as early as the second century AD. It was consistently used by the early church as an Affirmation of Faith at the time of baptism.

THE TESTIMONY OF THE CRITICS

It is of real interest to note that even the textual critics acknowledge the fact that there are no evidences that the Biblical references to the virgin birth are interpolated. Even though they may deny the fact of the virgin birth of our Lord, they have to admit that the Scriptural witness is part of the "original" writings! H.R. Mackintosh, well-known scholar and critic, makes the striking comment that "for history the really strong argument in favor of the virgin birth is the difficulty of accounting for the story otherwise than on the assumption of its truth."

"CONCEPTION" VERSUS "BIRTH"

It is well that we remind ourselves of the fact that conception and birth are not one and the same thing. Conception is an act on the part of the father whereby the seed of life is given, and birth is an act on the part of the mother whereby that partially developed life is ushered into the world. (See REGENERATION)

When we deal with conception, in this particular study, we are dealing with God as the Giver of the Seed of Life, for our Lord was "conceived by the Holy Spirit." When we deal with the birth of our Saviour, we are dealing with Mary who was simply the mother of the human body in which God tabernacled Himself. (See VIRGIN MARY)

THE "SEED OF THE WOMAN"

Turn in your Bible, if you will, to the Gospel according to Matthew. Chapter one begins with a genealogy: "the book of the generation of Jesus Christ, the Son of David, the Son of Abraham."

There is reason for this introduction which identifies our Lord with David the king and Abraham the Hebrew. The Jewish reader would immediately recognize one of the basic qualifications for Jesus as Messiah: namely that He is a descendent or "son" of David. Furthermore, as such, He is "The Seed" (singular) of the Promise given to Abraham. This, in turn, is related to the "Seed of the Woman" prophecy of Genesis 3:15 which speaks of Christ overcoming "that old serpent the devil." (Cf. Revelation 12:9 and our Study on SERPENT)

The apostle Paul, referring to the Seed of Abraham which is the "seed of the woman," says:

> "Now to Abraham and his Seed were the
> promises made. He saith not, and to seeds,
> as of many; but as of one: 'and to thy
> Seed' – which is Christ."   (Galatians 3:16)

As we have shown in our study of STARS as "signs" the promise concerning the "Seed" was given to the patriarch Abraham in connection with his enumerating the constellations along the path of the sun. (See Genesis 15) There can be no doubt that the 'seed' of Genesis 3:15 is Messiah who is proclaimed in the heavenly bodies (see STARS) as "the Seed of the woman." You will recall that God said to Abraham "So shall your seed be!" (Genesis 15:5)

The "woman" of Genesis 3:15 is a symbol of Israel, and the virgin Mary was the woman in particular through whom the "seed of Abraham" came. Matthew, having identified Jesus as a descendent of David and Abraham, then begins to list their key offspring. As you read the genealogy you will observe the reiterated "begat" (which speaks of conception) as David's royal line is traced. (You will note that the women listed are not spoken of as "begetting" sons, but only as wives of those who begat offspring. There is a reason for this, as we shall see. (Note verse 5)

THE "SHIFT" OF THE "BEGATS"

Now let your eye move down to the fifteenth verse of the first chapter of Matthew's Gospel. There we read these words:

> "And Eliud begat Eleazar, and
> Eleazar begat Matthen, and
> Matthan begat Jacob, and
> Jacob begat Joseph
>
> (the husband of Mary)
> of whom was born Jesus, who is called Christ."

Notice! For verse after verse we have the redundant ring of "begat," "begat," "begat." Suddenly, there in the midst of the steady pulse of this word, comes a "shift of gears." Here, instead of saying, "And Joseph begat Jesus," we are abruptly told that Joseph did not beget the Lord Jesus. This is accomplished in a subtle way by interrupting the established pattern.

Had Joseph been the father of Jesus by Mary, the apostle would carefully have used an already-established form of verse 5 ("And Salmon begat Boaz of Rahab; and Boaz begat Obed of Ruth." In other words Matthew would have written: "Jacob begat Joseph, and Joseph begat Jesus of Mary." (But, he didn't!)

Actually, as we shall see, Jesus had no father according to the flesh, and no mother according to the Spirit. He is the truly Unique Being of all human history, "born of woman" without being "conceived" by man. This is why the Lord Jesus Christ is prophetically called "seed of woman" in Genesis 3:15. Paul, referring indirectly to this passage as well as to the virgin birth, declares:

"But when the fullness of time was come,

God sent forth His Son, made of a woman. . ."

(Galatians 4:4)

A "SIGN" TO THE HOUSE OF DAVID

Turn in your Bible, please, to Isaiah 7:14. Let us see what the princely prophet has to say about the virgin birth. (Actually we ought to begin our reading at verse eleven). . .

"Ask thee a *sign* of the LORD thy God.

Ask it either in the depth, or in the heights!"

But Ahaz said,
"I will not ask, neither will I test the LORD."
And he said,
"Hear ye now, O House of David! Is it a small thing for you to weary men, but will ye weary my God also?
Therefore,
The LORD Himself shall give you a sign:
Behold,
A virgin shall conceive and bear a Son, and shall call His name 'Immanuel."

You will have observed already that this is a 'sign' and that it was to be given for the benefit of the House of David. . .the Jewish people. It cannot be said that an ordinary birth could qualify as a "sign" given by the LORD Himself!

In light of the controversy provoked by the publishing of the Revised Standard Version of the Bible, in which the words "young woman" are substituted for "virgin" (as in the King James Version), let us take a further look at the Hebrew of Isaiah 7:14.

"YOUNG WOMAN" VERSUS "VIRGIN"

The word rendered "virgin" in the KJV and "young woman" in the RSV is ALMAH. It is true that this Hebrew word means "a young woman of marriagable age." Such a meaning implies or expects virginity, but, of course, does not assure it. Furthermore, it indicates that the 'almah' is not married, although of sufficient age to enter into wedlock. Along this line of thinking, J. Gresham Machen, in his classical study on "The Virgin Birth of Christ" (Harper) writes:

"There is no place among the seven oc-
curances of ALMAH in the OT where the
word is clearly used of a woman who was
not a 'virgin.' It may readily be admitted
that ALMAH does not actually indicate
virginity, as does BETHULLAH; it means
rather "a young woman of marriagable age."
But on the other hand, one may well doubt,
in view of usage, whether it was a natural
word to use of anyone who was not in point
of fact, a virgin. C.F. Burney aptly compares
our English use of the words maiden and
damsel, terms which do not in themselves
connote virginity, yet would scarcely be
used of any but an unmarried woman."
(pages 288-9, opus cited)

TECHNICAL "PROOF" FOR VIRGIN

Actually the Lord, foreknowing that the time
would come when sceptical scholars would seek to
"take a swipe" (as the saying goes) at fundamental
Bible-believing Christians, actually provided a "proof"
text which plainly declares thats Isaiah 7:14 should
be rendered "virgin" rather than "young woman."

In Matthew 1:23 the Holy Spirit-directed apostle
declares that the virgin birth of Christ is a fulfillment
of Isaiah's prophecy! We read:

"Now all this was done, that it might be ful-
filled which was spoken of the Lord by the
prophet, saying, 'Behold, a virgin shall be
with child, and shall bring forth a son, and

they shall call his name Emmanuel,' which
being interpreted is 'God with us.'"

In this passage as it appears in the Greek New Testament the word ALMAH of Isaiah 7:14 is rendered
by the word PARTHENOS. This word is a technical
term for VIRGIN. It means "a young woman who has
never had intercourse with a man." Since the Word of
God plainly states that the virgin birth of Christ is
in fulfilment of Isaiah 7:14, and uses the technical
term for "virgin" to render the Hebrew word for AL-
MAH, it must be acknowledged that such is the true
interpretation!

GOD'S CURSE ON JECHONIAS

You have undoubtedly observed that the genealogy given in Matthew's gospel is that of Joseph, the
stepfather of Jesus. It must always be remembered that
every portion of Scripture is included for a specific
reason. This includes genealogies. We have already
seen that the abrupt change in established pattern of
the genealogy at hand indicates that Joseph was not
the father of Jesus (in addition to the fact that the
Bible clearly states that He was conceived by the Holy
Spirit and not man.) Now let us observe a second fact
which is revealed.

In Matthew 1:11 you will observe the cursed name
of Jechonias. I say "cursed" for a reason which will be
revealed in Scripture in a moment. Matthew says:

"And Josias begat Jechonias and his brethren, about the time they were carried away
to Babylon."

Compare this with I Chronicles 3:15-16 where the "sons" or descendents of King Josias are listed.

> "And the sons of JOSIAH were, the first-born, Johanan; the second JEHOIAKIM, the third, Zedekiah, the fourth Shallum. And the sons of JEHOIAKIM — JECONIAH his son, Zedekiah his son."

In other words the Jeconiah of Matthew 1:11 is what we would call a "grandson" of Josiah.

Sometimes our beloved KJV of the Scripture is confusing in that it spells the same name in different ways in different books of the Bible. This same man, Jechonias of Matthew 1:11, called Jeconiah in I Chron. 3:16, is called Coniah in Jeremiah 22:24 where he is carefully identified as:

> "Coniah, son of Jehoiakim, King of Judah".

Now we come to the verses which record the curse placed upon this man who was an ancestor of Joseph, "the husband of Mary, of whom was born Jesus." As we read verses 28 to 30 you will realize why Joseph could not possibly be the real father of our Lord since Jesus as Messiah, and descendent of David, will one day to sit on David's throne. We read:

> "Is this man Coniah a despised broken idol?
> Is he a vessel wherein is no pleasure?
> Wherefore are they cast out, he and his seed?
> Wherefore are they cast into a land which
> they know not?
> O earth, earth, earth! Hear the Word of the
>   LORD!

Write this man off as childless!
A man who shall not prosper in his days.
No man of his seed shall prosper,
sitting upon the throne of David, and
ruling any more in Judah."

Please take note of the fact that no descendent of
Coniah, (Joseph, the husband of Mary, being one),
would be allowed to sit on David's throne. If Jesus
had been conceived by Joseph, He, too, would be under the curse! How then does our Lord qualify to reign
as a true "Son of David?"

JESUS, "SON OF DAVID" BY MARY

The famous expositor, Lightfoot, quoting ancient
Rabbis, points out that they speak of Mary the mother
of Jesus in very reproachful terms, calling her the
"daughter of Heli." In Luke the word "son" is used
in much the same way that we do today, with reference to Joseph who is called a "son" of Heli (the
father of Mary). It is also stressed that Jesus was only
"supposedly" the "son of Joseph." Obviously he and
Mary were not going to talk to unbelieving neighbours
about the miraculous birth of her son!

If you will read the genealogy of Mary, given in
Luke three, you will discover that the Lord Jesus is a
"Son of David" by way of Nathan, avoiding the curse
placed upon Coniah. Furthermore, the genealogy continues back to Adam, "the son of God." This done to
emphasize the unique relationship sustained by Jesus
"born of woman" and true "Son of God."

It is not at all strange that a genealogy table of

our Lord existed in Luke's day. The Jews preserved these tables with remarkable accuracy throughout the centuries, especially if they had royal blood in their veins. After their return from the Babylonian exile the Jews again established their genealogical tables in the public record. It is a well-known fact that the famous Rabbi, Hillel, at the time of Christ, was able to prove himself to be a "son of David" from the public register. As descendents of the great king, Mary and Joseph would most naturally have kept careful records of their ancestry.

THE REAL ISSUE IS BEFORE YOU!

The real issue which lies before each of us is quite plain! You either believe the Word of God, or you do not!

The testimony of Scripture concerning the virgin birth of the Lord Jesus is clear cut. Not only is the fact stated openly and abruptly, but also by such gentle statements as "before they came together" and Joseph "knew her not." (Cf. Matthew 1:18-25)

Mary, too, was really surprised to hear the words of the angel of annunciation. Note her query:

"How shall this be, since I know not a man?"

She knew where babies come from, and, since she also knew her virginity to be a fact, she could not see how such a thing could take place! (Luke 1:31-34) In reply the messenger of God spoke plainly:

"The Holy Spirit shall come upon thee, and
The Power of the Highest (One) shall over-

shadow thee: therefore also that Holy Being which shall be born of thee shall be called the 'Son of God.'" (Luke 1:35)

Even the rank infidel must admit that the Bible does teach the doctrine of the virginbirth in plain language. If a man is indwelt by God the Holy Spirit he will say:

"Amen! Truth!" to the doctrine. Only the spirit of "that old Serpent, the Devil" mutters:

"HATH GOD SAID?"

Virgin Mary

IT IS NOT WITH ANY DESIRE to stir up controversy between Roman Catholics and Protestants that we have chosen the word "Mary" as our topic for today's broadcast, but with the desire to share with you certain Bible facts which will surely be helpful in sifting truth from fiction. Any thinking person knows that there is a fairly wide gulf between the theology of the Church of Rome (and the Eastern Orthodox) and the theology of the Bible Christian regarding the virgin mother of our Lord.

The Roman and Eastern Orthodox churches have a perfect right to proclaim their points of view, concerning what "The Church says," and we defend that right. In like manner, the Bible Christian has a perfect right to proclaim what "The Bible says" concerning Mary, the mother of Jesus. Each of us, naturally, has the responsibility to present what he believes to be Truth without a spirit of bitterness even while making his points with great firmness.

THE IMMACULATE CONCEPTION

Inasmuch as we lectured on the virgin birth last week, it is well that we begin our study of the word "Mary" with the analysis of the doctrine of the Immaculate Conception. This dogma was decreed by the Church of Rome on December 8, 1954, during the Pontificate of Pius IX, and states that:

"the doctrine which holds that the Most Blessed Virgin Mary at the first moment of her conception was, by singular grace and privilege of the Omnipotent God, in virtue of the merits of Jesus Christ, Saviour of the human race, preserved from all stain of original sin, is revealed by God and therefore to be firmly and resolutely believed by all the faithful."

(Dogmatic Bull "Ineffabilis Deus")

Commenting upon this doctrine, the Roman Pontiff, Pius XII, in his encyclical letter, "Fulgens Corona," wrote these words:

". . . it seems that the Blessed virgin Mary herself wished to confirm by some special sign the definition which the Vicar of her Divine Son on earth had pronounced admidst the applause of the whole Church. For indeed four years had not yet elapsed when, in a French town at the foot of the Pyrenees, the Virgin Mother, youthful and benign in appearance, clothed in a shining white garment, covered with a white mantle, and girded with a hanging blue cord, showed herself to a simple and innocent girl at the grotto of Massabielle. And to that same girl, earnestly inquiring the name of her with whose vision she was favored, with eyes raised to Heaven and sweetly smiling, she replied: "I am the Immaculate Conception.""

You may well ask, "What does the term 'Immaculate Conception' mean?" First of all let me remind you that it is not a synonym for 'Virgin Birth.' The term means that Mary, the virgin mother of Jesus, was, herself, conceived without sin. The word 'immaculate' is derived from two Latin words meaning "not stained." In other words this Roman doctrine states that Mary was born without a sin-nature. This, as we shall see, is one of many traditions which seeks to make the virgin mother equal with God the Son. He is "without sin" (though tempted in all points like as we), according to II Corinthians 5:21; Hebrews 4:15, 7:26; and I John 3:5, although all others have "sinned and come short of the glory of God." (Romans 3:23) Since He is without sin, Rome begins to establish the doctrine of the sin-less-ness of Mary, by the tradition of the 'Immaculate Conception.' (I say "tradition" because this admittedly is not Biblical revelation, but merely something the Pope had "revealed" to him.)

MARY A CONFESSED SINNER!

Only a sinner needs to call upon God to save him (or her) from sin, and this is precisely what the virgin Mary does in the opening words of her beautiful song known as the Magnificat, (recorded in Luke's Gospel, the first chapter, beginning with verse 46). Listen to her testament of Faith in the Saviour:

"My soul doth magnify the Lord, and my spirit doth rejoice in God *my Saviour!*"

Yes, Mary was just as much in need of a Saviour as

all of the rest of humanity, and she was saved by the "grace of God, through faith," in the same manner as all others who have called upon the Name of the Lord.

It has been said that the reason for the establishment of the doctrine of the Immaculate Conception was to answer the question, "How could Jesus be sinless (that is minus a sin nature) if he was born of a mother who possessed a sin nature?" This, of course, is a good question, but the Papal answer does not solve the problem. In fact it doubles it!

If Jesus could not be born without sin unless His mother was sinless, how could Mary be conceived by a sinful human father, and born of a sinful human mother? (After all she had twice as many parents with sin natures as did her son according to the flesh!) According to the flesh, our Lord had no father, so His problem involved only one parent. Mary's involves two sin-laden parents, so obviously backtracking one generation will not help! And, if you keep going back with the same device you will multiply the problem, and at last arrive at Eve!

Does it not stand to reason that if "by singular grace and privilege of the Omnipotent God" that Mary could be "preserved from all stain of original sin" that the Blessed Son of God could likewise? Obviously He could! The fact of the matter is that this device was used as one of a series of steps to exalt the virgin to a position as the equal of God the Son. Evidences abound in Scripture as to the sin-less-ness of our Lord but not one single verse testifies to the sin-less-ness of Mary. Only the opinion of a pope and the tradition of an organized church bear such a witness.

The Word of God is emphatically clear in its testimony that all men since Adam have sinned, missing the mark of the will of God through disobedience. The Scriptures plainly conclude all to be under sin with the sole exception of the Eternal Son of God. (Galatians 3:22) Bent upon fulfilling the will of the people who desire a goddess as well as a god, the Council of Trent in 1545 declined to allow that the "all" who have "sinned and come short of the glory of God" included the virgin Mary. (Cf. II Corinthians 5:21) Does it not seem reasonable that if Mary were sinless like Jesus there would be at least one verse in the Bible that openly declared it?

MARY, "THE MOTHER OF GOD"

The real fountainhead of Roman Mariolatry, however, is the heresy known as "Mary, Mother of God." From this Biblically heinous doctrine stem all of the teachings of the Roman and Eastern Church which seek to exalt the virgin as a goddess.

The term "Mother of God" (or 'theotokos' as it is called in the Greek Orthodox Church) was used for the first time during the Nestorian controversy, at the Council of Ephesus in AD 431. The friends of Nestorius, seeking to belittle the deity of our Lord, scoffingly cried: "If Christ is True God, then Mary must be the mother of God!" In their zeal to exalt Christ (in terms of His Spirit) as the Eternal Son of God, the orthodox turned the slander into a banner around which to rally.

THE PSEUDO-BASIS FOR THE DOCTRINE

Those who defend the "Mary, Mother of God" doctrine, seeking to honor her by urging the faithful to come "to God through Mary," resort to a number of un-Biblical arguments. Perhaps the most popular is the little invalid syllogism which goes like this:

1 – Jesus is God.
2 – Mary is the mother of Jesus, therefore
3 – Mary is the Mother of God!

On the surface this may seem logical to the untrained mind, but actually the conclusion is false because the first two statements are not compatible as to realm. Let me explain. The first statement is true in terms of the Spirit or True Being of Christ, but it is not a verity as far as His humanity is concerned. According to His Spirit the Lord Jesus is God the Son, while according to the flesh he is simply Jesus the man. It must be understood that the Lord Jesus had no father, according to the flesh, and no mother, according to the Spirit. The second statement is true in terms of the flesh, for Mary gave birth to the human body that He was here on earth. Humanity, however, is not God, for "God is Spirit."

Having said that, we face the fact that the first statement ("Jesus is God") is true only in the realm of the Spirit. The second statement ("Mary is the mother of Jesus") is true only in the realm of the flesh. Since "that which is born of the flesh is flesh, and that which is born of the Spirit is Spirit" (John 3:6) it is patent that the two realms are non-compatible, and, therefore, the third statement is false (namely that "Mary is the Mother of God.")

THE FOLLY OF THE DOCTRINE

The folly of the doctrine, if taken at all seriously, lies in the fact that if Mary were God's mother, then the Scriptures should read "In the beginning, Mary." The reality of the matter is that Mary was just an ordinary human being, self-confessed to be a sinner as we have already seen, who had a beginning in point of time, just as we. She is neither a goddess, nor the "mother of God," but simply a young Jewish virgin, named Mary, "of whom was born Jesus, called the Christ." (Cf. Matthew 1:16)

THE "CONCEPTION" OF CHRIST

When Jesus was "conceived" by God Who is Spirit, it was by means of the Seed of God which is declared to be the Word of God. (Luke 8:11) Mary responded in faith, and God brought His Word to pass, creating within her a human body for Himself (Cf. Hebrews 10:5) There was no act of copulation. This was a creative act by Divine Fiat. According to the flesh, the man Jesus had a point of beginning, "born of Mary." According to the Spirit, which is True Being, He was without beginning, for He existed in the beginning with God for He was and is God." (John 1:1-3)

Before we proceed any further, let me say that the basic difference between the theology of the Church of Rome and that of the born-again Christian is that occasioned by Final Authority. For the born-again Believer it is the Bible, The Word of God, which is his absolute and final Authority. For the faithful of the Church of Rome (as well as the Eastern Orthodox) it is the Church and its traditions which speak with the voice of Final Authority!

When a born-again Christian discovers that his church is preaching a doctrine contrary to Scripture, as is sometimes the case, he protests that the church is wrong because he knows the Bible is right. On the other hand, the faithful of the so-called Roman Catholic Church must accept the word of the Church as true. even if that word is diametrically opposed to clear, indisputable teachings of Scripture. (No one is questioning the "right" of each (humanly speaking) to decide for himself what his final authority will be. I am simply stating that this is the point from which the differences diverge.

MARY AS "CO-MEDIATOR"

There are many examples of what we mean when we say that the Church of Rome wilfully holds doctrines contrary to the plain teaching of Scripture. Consider the Romish doctrine of Mary as "Co-Mediator" with the Lord Jesus Christ. Rome declares that the "Way" to God is through Mary as well as Jesus, hence the slogan: "To God Through Mary."

Turn in your Bible (the Catholic Bible will do just as well as the Protestant!) to 1 Timothy 2:5. You will discover that the Word of God says that there is only "one mediator between God and men," and that mediator is a man (not a woman), and His dear name is "Christ Jesus" and not Mary! If the Bible is right, obviously the Church of Rome is wrong. Of course, as we have said, you must decide what is the final authority for your life. . .God. . .or the Church.

MARY AS "CO-REDEMPTRIX"

Another heresy, as far as the Bible-believing, born-again Christian is concerned, is the teaching of the Church of Rome that Mary is "Co-Redeemer" with Jesus. To "redeem" means "to purchase." According to Rome, the mother of Jesus is the Redeemer of the Church as well as the Lord. The Bible, however, says that we were "redeemed. . . with the precious blood of Christ, as of a lamb without blemish and without spot." (I Peter 1:18-19) Again and again He is declared to be the Redeemer (see the Word Key "REDEEM"), while the Bible never calls Mary "redeemer." Again you must decide what is the final authority of your life. . . God and the Bible. . . or Pope and the Church.

MARY, "SHE WHO CRUSHES SATAN"

Even though the Hebrew scholars of the Church of Rome know that the Hebrew text of Genesis 3:15 reads that "HE" shall bruise the head of the Serpent, still it is insisted that "SHE" will crush Satan. In the Douay Version of the Bible the passage is perverted to read:

"SHE shall crush thy head."

This, too, in spite of the fact that it is the overall teaching of the Catholic as well as Protestant Bibles, without exception, that Jesus is the Victor over Satan and never Mary! That Rome seeks to exalt Mary to a position of equality with Christ is clear as their very able spokesman, Bishop Sheen, says: "She can lift the fear, because her foot crushed the serpent of evil."

Of course, in this heresy, as in others, one must decide what is his final authority. . . the Word of God. . . or the Church of Rome.

MARY, "THE PERPETUAL VIRGIN"

Another anti-Biblical doctrine espoused by Rome is that Mary was a "perpetual virgin," that she had no other children (other than Jesus). The depicting of Joseph as an old man is purposefully designed to add credence to the heresy. That the perpetual virginity of Mary is false teaching, is easily proven by the Bible ("easily proven" as far as Bible-believers are concerned anyway!) That Psalm 69 is a Messianic Psalm is universally agreed upon. Verse 9 reads:

"I am become a stranger unto my brothers,
and an alien unto my mother's children."

The synonymous parallelism of the Hebrew poetry in this verse plainly declares that the "brethren" of the Messiah are the "children" of His mother! The Douay Version (Catholic) is just as plain. . .

"I am become a stranger unto my brethren,
an an alien to the sons of my mother."

In the Gospel accounts we see that the brothers of the Lord did not believe in Him. (Cf. Matthew 13:57, Mk. 6:4 and John 7:5)

The Greek word which is translated "brethren" is ADELPHOI which means "out of the same womb," and the same word with a feminine ending is used for

the word "sisters." (They were our Lord's half-broth-
ers and sisters since they shared the same mother, but
had different fathers.) Matthew 1:25 and Luke 2:7 indicate that Jesus was the first child to be born of
Mary, the normal implication being that others followed.

Not being aware of His virgin birth, the neighbors
were amazed at the mighty works of our Lord, saying:

"Is not this the carpenter's son? Is not his
mother called Mary? And his brothers,
James and Joses, and Simon, and Judas?"
(Again: the word translated "brethren" and "sisters"
is 'adelphoi,' and not the Greek word for "cousins.")

THE "ASSUMPTION OF MARY"

Another doctrine which seeks to make Mary the
equal of her Lord is that known as "The Assumption."
This dogma pronounces that "the Immaculate Mother
of God, ever virgin, when the course of her life on
earth was finished, was taken up body and soul into
heaven." This was necessary, of course, to make her
the equal of Christ in bodily resurrection without corruption. The Bible teaches that Christ never saw the
corruption of His flesh, but not one word about such
a miracle for Mary! (What is your Final Authority?)

MARY, "QUEEN OF HEAVEN"

"Queen of Heaven," a Babylonian name for Ishtar,
the mother goddess with the baby god in her arms, is
also applied to Mary by the Church of Rome. In the

Bible, however, (Jeremiah 7:18 and 44:17-19, 25) the "Queen of Heaven" provokes Jehovah to anger! Do you know that the word "Easter" comes from "Ishtar," and that the "hot cross buns" and "rabbits" of Romanism are copied from the worship of the accursed 'goddess' of ancient Babylon whose feast day was December 25? Could it be that just as Jesus declared that the Jews worshipped Satan under the name of Jehovah, that the Church of Rome is worshipping Ishtar, the goddess of fertility under the name of Mary? (Cf. John 8:41-44) Whom do you worship? Mary? Or the Son of God?

Wise Men

ONE OF THE MOST INTRIGUING stories in the world of literature, as well as in the record of the Gospels, is that given in the second chapter of the wonderful book of Matthew. Listen!

"Now when Jesus was born in Bethlehem of Judea in the days of Herod the king, behold, there came wise men from the east to Jerusalem, saying, 'Where is He who is born King of the Jews? For we have seen His star in the east, and are come to worship Him.' When Herod the king had heard these things, he was troubled, and all Jerusalem with him. And when he had gathered all the chief priests and scribes of the people together he demanded of them where Christ should be born. And they said unto him, 'In Bethlehem of Judea: for thus it is written by the prophet, And thou, Bethlehem, in the land of Judah, art not least among the princes of Judah, for out of thee shall come a Governor, Who shall rule My people Israel.' Then Herod, when he had privately called the wise men, inquired of them diligently what time the star appeared. And he sent them to Bethlehem, and said, 'Go and search diligently for the young Child; and when ye have found Him, being me word again, that I may come and worship Him also.' When

they had heard the King they departed,
and, lo, the star which they had seen in the
east, went before them until it came and
stood over where the young child was.
When they saw the star they rejoiced with
exceeding great joy. And when they were
come into the house, they saw the young
Child with Mary, His mother, and they
fell down and worshipped Him: and when
they had opened their treasures, they presented unto Him gifts: gold, and frank-
incense and myrrh. And being warned of
God in a dream that they should not return
to Herod, they departed into their own
country another way."

(Matthew 2:1-12)

WHO WERE THE WISE MEN?

As you read this beautiful story, does your mind
begin to visualize who these "wise men" were? Do
you know where they were from? Have you any idea
how they were dressed, or how they traveled? Why
would such personages make a journey to see a king,
and how on earth could a "star" lead them to the very
house in which the tiny infant lay? We shall seek to
answer these questions on the basis of both Biblical
and Historical facts in this study and the next. (Wise
Men, today, and Star of Bethlehem, next week.)

Our very first clue as to the identity of these "wise
men" is to be found in the phrase "wise men from the
east," in Matthew 2:1. The Greek word translated by
our two English words, "wise men," is MAGOI. We

observe that this word actually means "powerful or great (ones)." (The word SOPHOI in Greek means "wise ones," but that is not the word used here.)

The second part of our clue in this opening phrase is geographical, for they were "from the east." If you will examine any ancient map of the world, which shows national boundries during the time of Christ, you will discover one sprawling empire of very great strength: the fabulous Persian Empire. Not only was the empire greater as to land mass, but it was also equal to the Roman Empire in military might!

Now, let us take our Greek word MAGOI to any excellent encyclopaedia, and see if it has any connection with the Persian Empire to the east of Jerusalem. We shall discover that it most assuredly does!

THE "MAGOI" – RULERS OF PERSIA

The Magoi, who are called "the wise men" in our King James Version of the Bible, were actually very important figures in the government of ancient Persia. The Persians had a governing body known as Megistanes which was divided into two houses. The upper house members were called Magoi ("powerful ones") and the lower house members were called Sophoi or "wise ones."

The "wise men" of our Christmas Story are actually the Powerful Ones who ruled over Persia in the time of Christ. Furthermore, history also tells us that the Magoi were an aristocratic class of priests who were the king-makers of their empire!

WHY THEIR INTEREST IN CHRIST?

You may well ask, "Why were such powerful rulers interested in Christ?" That is a good question, and the answer is one of the most surprising pieces of information I have ever dug up in my studies!

You will remember, of course, that the Northern Kingdom of Israel was taken captive by the Assyrians over seven hundred years before Christ, carrying off thousands of captives. One hundred and thirtyfive years later the Babylonians, under Nebuchadnezzar, had overcome the Assyrians and had taken Jerusalem captive. The choice men and women and youth of the Southern Kingdom, which had been faithful to the Davidic throne (Judah and Benjamin) were then scattered throughout the Babylonian Empire.

Because the Jew knew the Bible doctrine which commands the people of God to obey those in authority over them, even though it be an alien power, these deportees were so obedient and dependable that they soon began to be trusted with important offices. One has only to think of Joseph, vice-regent of Pharaoh, and Daniel, to see how the application of the doctrine "turned out." It is an established fact that during the Parthian Dynasty, which ruled in the time of Christ, many of the Magoi could trace their ancestry back to Abraham through the Babylonian and Assyrian captivities. Obedient to government they had been counted so worthy of trust that they eventually ruled the very people who had been their captors!

This, of course, answers our question. The Magoi were interested in the birth of Christ because these particular "wise men" were sons of Abraham and had some knowledge of prophecy concerning the "Coming One" who was to sit on David's throne in Jerusalem.

HOW MANY MAGOI WERE THERE?

By the way, can you find the verse where it tells us just how many Magoi there were? Does the Bible say that there were three? No, it does not. All we know from the Scripture account is that there were two or more (since the 'oi' ending indicates plurality). The idea of "three wise men" has come down to us from the traditional children's fairy tales that have attached themselves to the Christmas story. Actually there is reason to believe that there were quite a few of these august personages who made their way over desert wastes to see the Christ Child.

On the walls of one of the catacombs of Rome there is a primitive painting of the Magoi. They are part of a very large entourage of soldiers who obviously served as their body guard. (One can hardly imagine Eastern monarchs traveling all alone from Persia to Judea!)

HOW DID THE MAGOI TRAVEL?

Perhaps you have observed the fact that the artists are in disagreement about the mode of transportation used by the VIP's from Persia. Some show Arabs on camel back, while others depict them as kings with European-style crowns, astride horses. Which group is right (if either)? Actually neither is completely correct, as we shall see.

The ancient historians tell us something about the use that the Persians made of horses and camels that solves the question. These people were the most fantastic equestrians, and they had the finest cavalry the world has ever known. Naturally, whenever any of their national leaders made trips to a foreign country (such as Palestine), these crack cavalry units were with them. With mounted troops and personal servants to the Magoi, there were bound to be hundreds of men in the party. . . not three lonely travelers!

It also might be noted that the Persians used the camel only as a baggage bearer. We can be sure that no mighty ruler of an empire the equal of Rome would make a journey abroad astride a lowly camel!

WHAT DID THE MAGOI WEAR?

Not only does the painting on the catacomb wall reveal the fact that the "wise men" were part of a very large entourage, but it also tells us something about the kind of clothing they wore. And. . . you guessed it. . . they wore neither the burnoosed garb of arabs nor the ermine-tipped robes of European monarchs! The dress is phrygian (conical hats and short capes) and decidedly that of Oriental Poetentates. This, of course, we would expect since they were "from the East," and not from the West.

WHY WAS HEROD "TROUBLED?"

This leads us to ask the question why the Scripture says that Herod was "troubled, and all Jerusalem with him." (Matthew 2:3) Historical facts again come to

our aid. First of all he had what would amount to a
small army at the gates of Jerusalem, and one that
was internationally known as a fierce fighting force
of formidable power. In the second place most of the
Jerusalem garrison at Herod's disposal was quelling
a revolt in Armenia. In the third place the land of
Palestine had long been a buffer state between the
great Roman Empire in the West, and the gargantuan
Persian Empire to the East. Since Jerusalem was, at
that time, under the sway of Rome, the appearance of
a large cavalry unit from Persia could spell trouble!
In the fourth place Herod had seen Perisans before. . .
(or, perhaps, it would be better to say he had seen
them "behind!" because some thirty years before he
had hightailed it for Rome with the Persian cavalry at
his heels!) Once in the city set on seven hills Herod
had cried out for help from his friends Mark Anthony
and Caesar Augustus to have the Senate proclaim him
"king of the Jews," as well as to provide a garrison
large enough to hold his position. In the fifth place,
the despised Idumean Arab now heard the awful news
that there was a Contender to the Throne, One who
was not a puppet king by appointment, like Herod who
was vigorously hated by the people, but a Monarch by
birth! If word of this got around to the populace there
could be an insurrection, for the Jews were full
of intense longing for the coming Messiah-King. He
was agitated for one set of reasons, and the people
were in a tumult for another! It was an exciting and
tense moment for all concerned.

THE METHOD IN HEROD'S MADNESS

Herod, however, in a time of crisis, knew when to yield as well as when to resist. He was an astute politician, as well as hardened soldier. Obviously, he was in no position to argue the presence of the Magoi with their military might, with his garrison depleted. Furthermore, he observed their keen interest in the One who was "born king of the Jews" and knew that any show of resistance on his part would incur their displeasure. There was but one thing to do. Treat them with a great show of cooperation, feigning keen interest in their project, while assuring them that he, too, would delight in falling prostrate before Messiah the Prince. Hence his deceitful words:

> "Go and search diligently for the young Child; and when you have found Him, bring me word again, that I may come and worship Him also."

> (Matthew 2:8)

Of course, as succeeding events indicate, Herod purposed only to discover the whereabouts of this infant contender to his throne, that he might dispose of him before he could ever grow up to rule. (Cf. Matt. 2:13-16)

THE REAL "WISDOM" OF THE MAGOI

It may be true that the word "wise men" is a poor translation of the Greek word MAGOI, but we certainly can see that these powerful potentates were very,

very wise. They did something that the scribes, with their superior knowledge of the Scriptures failed to do — they followed the light they had! The priesthood as well as the scribes, knew what "the Bible says" about the place of Messiah's birth, but neither group showed the slightest interest in rushing down to little Bethlehem to greet Him! What an amazing thing! The leaders of Israel hear of the birth of the longed-for Christ, tell the king makers from afar where they can find the Child, and go back to their intrigue and co-existence with a king they despised! The Magoi, on the other hand, as Persian Jews with limited knowledge of the Holy Scriptures, have gone "all out" to find the Christ Child that they might bring Him gifts and worship Him. Their faith was such that it demanded action when His "sign" appeared to them. We do not have space in this study to take up the nature of the "sign" of Messiah which is popularly called "the Star of Bethlehem," but we shall do so in our broadcast of next week. (See STAR OF BETHLEHEM)

THEY WORSHIPPED CHRIST, NOT MARY

Another fact which indicates the wisdom of the Magoi is the fact that they worshipped Christ but not His mother. (Matthew 2:11) Unfortunately we live in the midst of so many corrupt forms of Christianity that the worship of the creature rather than the Creator is not only tolerated in some churches, but encouraged! (Cf. Romans 1:25) The gifts of the "wise men" were not for Mary, but for the One whom the

Holy Spirit identified as "the Son of God." Those
cults which encourage the veneration of Mary, calling
her the Queen of Heaven, Co-Redeemer, Co-Mediator,
Sinless One, etc., not only show themselves to be less
wise then the Magoi but worshippers of the creature
rather than the Creator. Matthew specifically states
that:

> "They fill down, and *worshipped HIM;*
> and when they had opened their treasures,
> they presented *unto Him gifts; gold,*
> frankincense, and myrrh."
>
> (2:11)

The reason that they worshipped Him was because He
is Emmanuel, "God with us" (1:23). Any careful
student of Scripture knows that the Deity or Godhood
of Jesus Christ is plainly taught. He is supposed to be
the object of our worship. (Cf. Colossians 1:16) As
a creature of God, regardless of how pure and lovely
Mary may have been (and surely was), she is not a
goddess, and the Magoi knew it. They were, indeed,
"wise men" of the highest order.

YOUR GIFT FOR HIM

There is an old English Hymn which expresses so
beautifully the true manner of gift-bringing which is
to characterize the "wise men" of the Church Age.

The WISE may bring their learning,
The RICH may bring their wealth,
And some may bring their greatness,
And some bring strength and health;

They, too, would bring their treasures
To offer to the King!
They have no wealth or learning. . .
What shall the children bring?

    We'll bring Him hearts that love Him,
    We'll bring Him thankful praise,
    And young souls meekly striving
    To walk in holy ways!

    And these will be the treasures
    We offer to the King;
    And these the Gifts that even
    The poorest child may bring!

We'll bring the little duties
  We have to do each day;
    We'll try our best to please Him
      At home, at school, at play:

And better are these treasures
  To offer to the King,
    Than richest gifts without them!
      Yet these a child may bring."   AMEN.

May I suggest to you how you may indeed bring a wise gift to the Christ Child? Simply give Him your heart. Totally. . . unreservedly. . . to rule as King.

Star Of Bethlehem

STARS AND PLANETS have always held a fascination for man. As we have already seen in our study of the stars as "signs," it is apparent that the holy prophets and apostles all felt that the heavenly bodies offered man much more than just beauty and illumination in the physical realm. They, like Moses, knew that the lights in the heavens were established as "signs" which pointed to Truth. We should not be surprised, therefore, to discover that great significance is attached to the "Star of Bethlehem."

"STAR" USED IN A BROAD SENSE

We ought to begin by observing the fact that the term "star" was used very loosely by the ancients for any and all luminaries observed in the atmosphere above the earth or in outer space. All of the heavenly bodies and all astral phenomena, including comets and planets, were "lumped together" under the category of "stars." This fact both complicates and simplifies in measure the task which is ours — searching out just what the Bible means by the term "His star" which we commonly call "the star of Bethlehem."

"STARS" IN THE OLD TESTAMENT

There are a number of direct references to the celestial bodies in the Old Testament. Job heard God speak of the morning stars singing together (38:7).

Moses knew that God was the Creator who spoke the heavenly lights into existence (Genesis 1:16), and the Psalmist considered the stars to be fashioned by the "fingers" of God (Psalm 8:3). It is also apparent that the latter understood that it was Jehovah who gave the stars their names (Psalm 147:4). Of course the very fact that many of the constellations bear the very same names, in different languages, throughout the world verifies the fact that there was originally one source for them all. Several constellations are mentioned in Scripture. There is Arcturus (the Great Bear), and Orion and the Pleiades (sometimes called "the seven stars"). (Cf. Job 9:9; 38:31f; and Amos 5:8) There are, of course, many other allusions to the testimony of stars to the glory of the Creator.

WORSHIP OF CELESTIAL BODIES A SIN

Inasmuch as the ancients understood that the lights in the heavens were "signs" which stood for the Person and Work of the Coming One, it was necessary that God should command them not to worship them. Since the Egyptians and other pagan peoples of Palestine, Phoenicia, and the northern coast of Africa had turned from the worship of the Creator to the adoration of the creature, Jehovah gave specific insturctions to Israel:

> "And lest thou lift up thine eyes unto heaven, and when thou seest the sun, the moon, and the stars, even all the host of heaven, and shouldest be driven to worship, and serve them which the LORD thy God

hath divided unto all nations under the
whole heaven."

(Deuteronomy 4:19)

In spite of the warnings, however, Israel did worship
the "signs" in the heavens from time to time, rather
than the Coming One (the Messiah) to whom they
pointed. Examples of this are to be seen in their worship of the sun and the solar disc, plus various animal
deities which were venerated by their pagan neighbors.
(Cf. II Kings 17:16; 21:3; 23:5; Jeremiah 19:13;
Amos 5:26; Zepheniah 1:5; Acts 7:42-43 and Romans
1:18-32) Like her enemies, Israel often fell to ven-
erating the creature rather than the Creator, the
physical lights in the heavens rather than the One
Who is "The Light" to whom the heavens point.

ANCIENT STAR–SUPERSTITIONS

As one reads the various comments of preachers
and popes, astronomers and agnostics, concerning the
identity of the Star of Bethlehem, he is amazed to
see that just about everything which has ever flashed
over the earth has been called "His star." For example,
Origen of Alexandria, who, about the year 200 AD.
was well-known throughout the church had some
ideas about the Star of Bethlehem. He wrote:

"I am of the opinion that the star which
appeared to the Wise Men in the East was a
new star which had nothing in common with
those stars which appear either in the firmament or in the lower levels of the atmos-

phere. It belonged (presumably) to the category of those celestial fires which appear from time to time, and to which the Greeks have given names according to their shape, such as Comets, Firey Beams, Starry Hosts, Starry Tails, or Vessels, or some such name."

This "opinion" on the part of Origen had its effect on the popular mind and is reflected in the art work of succeeding generations, as may be seen in the "spray tails" and comets on our Christmas cards of today.

Although such notions have no Biblical basis, the superstitions of the masses encouraged their acceptance. For example, when the ancients saw a comet or "shooting star" blaze through the heavens, they believed that it marked the death or birth of some great person. When Julius Caesar was assassinated shortly after the "Ides of March" in 44 BC there was a brilliant comet observed throughout the night by the peoples of the Roman Empire. They were quite confident that the "star" marked Caesar's death.

Even in our enlightened age of reason there is always someone in the news media who relates political and religious happenings to astral activities. In 1910, the appearance of Halley's Comet was thought by many to be the reappearance of the Star of Bethlehem! This year, when an unnamed shooting star made its appearance in the firmament, several newspapers had articles relating it to "His star." Such conjectures reveal an abysmal ignorance of Scripture, or else the total lack of logic in putting together the obvious facts given in Matthew's account.

THE ASTRONOMER'S THEORY

One of the most intriguing theories now being advanced by persons of scientific bent is that developed by Johannes Kepler. In many planetariums throughout the world, during the Advent Season, astronomers are giving a "logical explanation of the Star of Bethlehem." Like the superstition theories, the scientific theory breaks down in the light of the Scripture account. However, since this particular theory is so widely accepted as plausible, let us take a moment to examine it and see why it will not "hold water" (as the saying goes).

As we have said there was an astronomer by the name of Johannes Kepler who developed the theory so popular with planetarium operators. He was the royal astronomer of Prague, and, as a person, a mixture of mystic and mathematician. One December night, high up in his observatory overlooking the Moldau, Kepler observed the conjunction of two planets in the constellation Pisces. Those two planets were Saturn and Jupiter. Christmas was just a week away, and the proximity of the birthday of Messiah and this rendevous of Saturn and Jupiter in Pisces stirred Kepler to remembrance of some ancient rabbinical writings.

According to Abarbanel, one of the old rabbinical writers, the Jews believed that Messiah would come at a time when there was a conjunction of Saturn and Jupiter in the constellation Pisces. This superstition was based on the popular notion that Jupiter was the planetary sign of royalty, and Saturn the "protecting power of Israel." For them the stars were often thought of as related to spirit beings, such as angels, who were striving for or against the people of God. (Cf. Judges 5:20) They also remembered that it is taught in Scripture that the Great Deliverer of the Jewish people is to be as a "Star out of Jacob." (Cf. Numbers 24:16-17) Furthermore, the Chaldeans are said to have believed that the constellation Pisces was the particular sign of Palestine.

Abarbanel thought, therefore, that the conjunction of Saturn ("Israel's Protector") and Jupiter (the sign of royalty or kingship) in Pisces (Palestine) just might be understood by the Magoi as meaning that Israel's Messiah and King had been born. Since the capitol of the little country of Israel was Jerusalem, it would be natural for the Magoi to go there first.

As Royal Astronomer Johannes Kepler mused upon these ancient writings of Abarbanel, he was spurred to make some mathematical calculations to see if this same conjunction could have taken place in the year of our Lord's birth. His figuring determined that there was a three-fold conjunction of Saturn and Jupiter in the constellation Pisces in the year 7 BC.

Kepler's theory about the Star of Bethlehem being formed by the conjunction of Saturn and Jupiter in the constellation Pisces passed by quite unnoticed for a number of years. This was partially due to the fact that the calculated conjunction was in the year 7 BC. However, as time went by, a number of persons pointed out that this posed no problem since our modern calendar is inaccurate by seven years! This happened when a Scythian monk by the name of Dionysius Exigus was instructed in the sixth century of the Christian era to make a calendar. He made several mistakes.

He forgot to compute the year zero. Nor did he take into account the four years when Caesar Augustus ruled under his own name of Octavian. Finally he did not include the two years of his joint reign making a total of seven years error. Herod the King who sought the life of the Infant Jesus died in 4 BC, according to the erroneous reckoning of our modern calendar, and all babies "two years old and under, according to the time which Herod had diligently inquired of the Wise Men," were slaughtered, plus the death of the wicked king, totals seven years of calendar error.)

KEPLER'S PROJECTIONS CONFIRMED

The real problem in the Kepler theory, therefore, was not in the date of 7 BC, but in the fact that no one knew whether his mathematical projections of where the stars would be in the heavens in a time long past, could really be trusted. In 1925, however, a German scientist by the name of Schnabel, deciphered some Neo-Babylonian tablets found in the Royal School of Astronomy in ancient Sippar, Babylon. One of these clay records stated that there had been a three-fold rendevous of Saturn and Jupiter in Pisces in the very year, and on the very days projected by Kepler! This not only added credence to the Bohemian's theory of the Star of Bethlehem, but affirmed his laws of planetary motion which bear his name until this day.

Modern astronomers, using the very latest techniques for "rolling back the celestial clock", agree that the three-fold conjunction which must have looked very much like a hugh star on the sky line, actually occurred. According to modern astronomers, and Kepler, the schedule of conjunctions is as follows: The first took place on May 29th, and was visible on the morning horizon for about two hours. The second encounter of Jupiter and Saturn in Pisces took place on October 3rd, and the final appearance was on December 4th — all in the year 7 BC. (It is of keen interest to note that the middle date, October 3rd, was the "Day of Atonement" for the Jews in that year.) Josephus, the Hebrew historian, adds that about this time there was a popular rumor abroad that the rule of Rome was about to be terminated because many had seen a "sign" from heaven announcing Messiah's coming!

THE STAR "WENT BEFORE THEM"

Everything seems so logical about this theory, so far, but how about the statement that the star "went before them" to Bethlehem? Do the astonomers have any solution to the problem as to how a star on the horizon could go before the Magoi as they went down to Bethlehem? Their answer is "Yes!" It seems that the third conjunction of Saturn and Jupiter in Pisces would have been on the horizon South West of Jerusalem, fusing into a huge blazing orb beyond Bethlehem. It all seems to fit, doesn't it? But, wait! There is one more important question which is yet unanswered. Let's go back to the Scripture to see a very interesting statement which positively rules out the so-called "scientific" theory expounded by the astonomers in their attempt to give credence to the Bible account of the "star" which led the Wise Men to Christ. Look at Matthew 2:9 and observe that it says that the 'star'

"stood over where the young child was."

Now, it is impossible for a star to "go before," (being on the horizon), and to "stand over" a house or even a village at one and the same time! Furthermore a star standing over Bethlehem would also appear to be over Jerusalem at the same instant, and it surely could not mark one house as being the place "where the young Child was"! Finally, the Scripture declares that the star actually "went" (that is moved along) before them on the way to the City of David.

WHAT SAYS THE THEORIES?

Before we go any further, let us take a moment to recapitulate what we have said about the various superstitions and theories, foolish and profound, which have attached themselves to Matthew's story of the Star of Bethlehem.

First of all there is the old idea that the "star" was actually a comet which blazed across the sky. Surely it is obvious by now that this is not the answer. A shooting star might point in the direction of Bethlehem but it could never "stand over" a house as a marker! Not only that, if it did stop over a house at a distance close enough to show which one was the dwelling of the Christ Child, it would burn the place to a crisp! No, the Star of Bethlehem was no comet!

In the second place, as we have seen, the "scientific" theory which is so popular among planetarium operators, and which has come down to us from the fertile brain of Johannes Kepler, will not stand the scrutiny of Scripture. The conjunction of Saturn and Jupiter in the constellation Pisces in the year in which the Lord Jesus was born may have been taken to be a "sign" of Messiah's birth by many Jews, but it cannot meet the demands of Scripture. Such a rendevous in outer space makes it impossible for said planets and stars to move down the twisting road to Bethlehem, or to hover over a house, to single it out from among the rest of the homes in the little Judean village! Imagine Jupiter and Saturn in Pisces accomplishing such a feat without the earth disintegrating!

WHAT SAY THE SCRIPTURES?

Having examined the more plausible of the theories which have come to us from ancient, medieval, and modern times, and having seen that they simply will not "hold water" when compared with Scripture, let us approach our problem from another position. It is not sufficient to debunk the theories of others. We must at least make an attempt to give an answer as to what the Star of Bethlehem was, if we are to be fair. Furthermore, we must be willing to examine our own answer by the same acid test of "What says the Word of God?" In other words our 'star' must be identified easily as a valid Messianic "sign," and it must meet the requirements which demand that it actually go "before" the Magoi, leading them the way to Bethlehem, and actually stand "over" the specific house in which the Holy Infant lay.

THE "SIGN" OF THE MESSIAH

Actually, in the Church's anxiety to provide an acceptable statement as to the identity of the Star, the very, very obvious answer has been overlooked. Just pause for a moment and think of what the Bible says about the phenomena which is the "sign of the Son of Man"and His coming to earth. It is the same amazing blaze of glory which marked the Presence of Jehovah in the midst of Israel during their journey through the wilderness, "leading them the way". It was a phenomena which not only went 'before them," as in the case of the Star of Bethlehem, but it also marked the residence of the Son of God in a goat hair tent as He communed with Moses from between the Cherubim over the Mercy Seat. Not only did it "mark" the place where the Son of God dwelt, but it also rested on a dwelling which ordinary "stars" would have burned. Whether it was over the tabernacle, or a bush which was not consumed, or upon Mount Sinai, it always declared one thing: "God is present in this place."

THE 'STAR' IS THE FIREY PILLAR

By now you surely have guessed what the Star of Bethlehem was. Yes! It was the Shekinah Glory or Pillar of Fire which was Jehovah's "sign" to the Jew that He was present. The Hebrew Magoi (See WISE MEN) would have recognized it immediately as the "sign" of Messiah's coming or presence (See study on PAROUSIA), and if fulfills the demands of the narrative in Matthew for a heavenly body which both goes before the Magoi and rests upon the place where the young Child lay.

THE "STAR" IS COMING AGAIN

May I quietly remind you that the Star of Bethlehem is going to be seen again? It is the "sign of the Son of Man," the glory cloud, which will announce His second Coming," and it may be soon!" (Cf. Matthew 24:30) When He ascended into heaven it was in the cloud of the glory. When He comes again it will be in the cloud of the glory. (In the first instance the term "cloud" is used because it was by day. At the Second Coming in power and great glory it will be in the firey cloud, because all will be dark.)

Salvation

THE DOCTRINE OF SALVATION is one of the most glorious key words of Scripture. It is a multi-faceted doctrine which, the more perfectly it is comprehended, will thrill your heart again and again as you probe its unlimited treasures.

As the student examines the key words of the Bible he observes that there are several great doctrines which are directly related to salvation. In each the cross is central. Our salvation is grounded in the preciousness of the shed blood of the Mediator since it is the purchase price by which we are Redeemed—the Gift beyond measure by which the Father has been Propitiated—the divine Sum by which man's account has been eternally Reconciled on God's books—the magnificent balance of Divine Righteousness credited to the Believer's account. Apart from these "mighty works" of Christ on our behalf there would be no "so great salvation."

THE N.T. GREEK TERM

The Greek word for SALVATION is 'soteria'. From this term comes (by transliteration) our English word 'soteriology.' Soteriology is the study of the doctrine of salvation. The root word is 'soter' which means "saviour" or "deliverer." Soteria appears some 45 times in the pages of the Greek New Testament. In forty instances it is translated "salvation," while its other five appearances are rendered by such words as "saved" (Luke 1:71 and Romans 10:1), "deliver" (Acts 7:25), "health" (Acts 27:34) and "saving" in Hebrews 11:7.

"SALVATION" IN THE O.T.

Our key word, salvation, is used of deliverance in the physical as well as the spiritual realm in the Old Testament. In the physical realm, assurance is given the People of God that He will give them victory over their enemies if they will but occupy the land in obedience. In the spiritual realm, there is divine assurance that Jehovah has provided a Way for them to establish a right relationship with their God which results in deliverance from His wrath.

"SALVATION" DEFINED

The basic meaning of the word SALVATION, in the New Testament as well as the Old, is "deliverance from harm to safety." This deliverance or salvation is always by the "mighty arm" or power of Jehovah in spite of the total inability of the delivered one to save himself. Salvation is a picture word which communicates the ideas of "wholeness, restoration, safety, healing, and preservation (as well as deliverance).

THE "TENSES" OF SALVATION

There is an interesting story told about the venerable Bishop Moule and an encounter he had with a Salvation Army lassie on the streets of Durham, England in the latter part of the nineteenth century. The young girl stopped him rather abruptly and said: "Sir, are you saved?" With a winsome smile and a twinkle in his eye the grand old Bible scholar replied: "Lassie, do you mean have I BEEN saved, or am I BEING saved, or shall I yet BE saved?" Then, in a most gracious manner, the aged Bishop proceeded to explain to the simple lass that God, in Christ, had provided a salvation for us sinners that encompasses far more than deliverance from the Lake of Fire. It is salvation from the penalty of sin which alienated us from our Creator, to complete restoration to Him. It is deliverance from the dominion or rule of sin to the rule or dominion of the indwelling Holy Spirit. It is salvation from even the presence of sin, in a day yet to come, unto a position of eternal safety from all evil, debilitating forces. In short, the Bishop told the Salvation Army lassie, Salvation is the continuous work of deliverance by the One who was named Jesus, because He saves His people from their sins. (Matt. 1:21.)

From God's standpoint as the One who is time-less and who dwells in eternity, it is true that our salvation was accomplished once and for all whom the Father predetermined to save. On the other hand, from the point of view of the Elect whose days are reckoned in terms of the passage of time, it helps to use the "tenses" by which we describe time. Let us remember, however, that "salvation" is a continuous process of deliverance and not something that happens at a given point in time and then is all over with.

"SALVATION" IN THE "PAST TENSE"

Let me explain what I mean. In terms of human time it may be said that the born-again Believer WAS saved, past tense, from the Penalty of sin. As far as his entering into the experience of salvation is concerned it began the moment he accepted Jesus Christ as his personal Lord and Saviour. In that moment it became an accepted fact that he no longer need fear the terror and torment of the Lake of Fire, for his unrighteousness had been "sent away" and the very righteousness of God had been put to his account.

Furthermore, in terms of the "past tense" of salvation, it will be seen that it is related to the rarely understood doctrines of election and predestination as well as the more intimate doctrines of faith, reconciliation, propitiation, justification, substitution, and redemption. For example: In eternity past the doctrine of salvation joins with the doctrines of predestination and election within the framework of the absolute foreknowledge of God. In the past tense, at the point in time when the Lamb of God was offered up as the divine Sacrificial Victim, the doctrine of salvation joins with the doctrines of propitiation, reconciliation, substitution and redemption. Then ,in terms of that moment past when you first believed on the Son of God as your Lord and Saviour, the doctrine of salvation joined with the doctrines of faith and justification. These points of interlocking doctrines are not to be thought of as absolute and unyielding, but only as suggested points of inter-involvement.

EXPERIENTIAL "SALVATION"

Since most people think of salvation in terms of an "experience," let us look at it from that point of view for just a moment. Experientially speaking you were "saved" the moment that you put your faith in Jesus as your personal Saviour and divine Lord. A good example of this is seen in the promise of God to the Philippian jailer, through Paul and Silas. In Acts 16: 30-31 we hear his cry, "Sirs, what must I do to be saved?" Then comes that glorious reply, "Believe on the Lord Jesus Christ, and thou shalt be saved and thy household." Salvation, in the sense of time and experience, is said to be his upon his acceptance of Jesus Christ as Lord. Salvation, then, becomes "ours" experientially the moment we trust in the Lord Jesus.

Another illustration of salvation related to a point in time past is to be seen in Luke 7:50. There we read of Jesus speaking to the sinful woman who had anointed   His feet in the house of Simon. You will recall that He said to her, "Thy faith hath saved thee! Go in peace!" At the moment that she exercised her trust in Him she was saved from the penalty of sin in spite of her unrighteousnesses. This is why Paul, in Romans 4:5, says:

> "But to him that worketh not,
> but believeth on Him who justifies the ungodly,
> his faith is counted for righteousness!"

SALVATION "FROM" AND "UNTO"

We have already indicated that salvation is actually a "process" and not just an "event." That which was "begun" in you as God's "good work" is guaranteed to one day be finished in the Day of Christ Jesus. In terms of eternity past it was as good as completed in the Mind of Christ, but, in terms of historical time and personal experience, it will not be finished until we receive our resurrection bodies. (Cf. Phil. 1:6)

In this process we see that we are not just being saved "from" the Lake of Fire, but, also, "unto" heaven. "God so loved the world that He gave His only begotten Son, that whosoever believeth in Him should not perish, but have everlasting Life."

By faith in Jesus as Saviour and Lord we are saved FROM "perishing" and UNTO "Life eternal." It is a divine "process" away from incompleteness unto completeness; from being lost to being found; from sickness to health; and from hell to heaven. (Cf. II Corinthians 2:15) We were delivered in spite of ourselves by the grace of God without any effort or "good works" on our part as other word studies will show.

We must insist that you recognize that the Bible teaches very plainly that salvation is a "process" and not just an "event." This is nowhere more apparent than in Matthew 1:21 where the angel instructs Joseph, saying, "Thou shalt call His name JESUS, for He shall save His people from their sins." Now please observe that the angel does not say that our Lord will save His people from the Lake of Fire, but "from their sins."

If you have "BEEN" saved, past tense, from the Penalty of sin, then you are now "BEING" saved from the rule of dominion of sin. I know that there are misguided individuals who are lacking in a knowledge of Bible doctrine who think that they have had a "past tense" experience of salvation in which they were completely cleansed so that they are now without sin. Any person with a knowledge of the Scriptures knows, however, that the Word of God specifically states:

> "If we say that we have no sin
> we deceive ourselves
> and The Truth (Jesus Christ)
> is not in us."   I John 1:8

SALVATION IN THE "PRESENT TENSE"

Remembering that our salvation was an accomplished fact in the mind of God in terms of His foreknowledge whereby the Lord knows the end from the beginning, we may still relate ourselves to our salvation in terms of time and experience. While doing so let us be sure to keep in mind that our deliverance from sin is a "process" and that we who HAVE BEEN saved from the Penalty of sin are BEING saved from the dominion of sin.

Furthermore, as we study all of the doctrines related to our salvation we shall see that the Elect have absolutely nothing to do with getting themselves saved or with keeping themselves saved. He, not we, is the Saviour. Even our "faith" (as we shall see in the

analysis of that key word) is His work and not ours.
This is why the apostle Paul declares:

> "For by grace are ye saved through faith,
> and that not of yourselves,
> it is the Gift of God:
> not of works lest any man should boast."
> (Ephesians 2:8-9)

As far as the heirs of Life Eternal are concerned, the
"good works" of the past had nothing to do with getting them saved any more than their "good works" in
the present or future have with keeping them saved!
We are not suggesting for a moment that "good works"
are unimportant, or that "bad works" are to be fli-
pantly engaged in. By no manner of means. As Paul
would say, when discussing this very matter.

> "Shall we continue in sin that grace may
> abound? God forbid!" (Romans 6:1)

No, what we are saying is that you are not saved from
the Penalty of sin by your "good works," nor can you
lose your salvation by subsequent "bad works." You
yourself have no more to do with KEEPING yourself
saved than you did with GETTING yourself saved!
Paul, again, makes this patently clear in First Corinthians 3:11-15 where he talks about the various kinds
of "works" which a Christian may build on Christ. As
the Believer stands before God to be judged he may
suffer the loss of all rewards, and all of his works
may go up in smoke, but "he himself shall be saved."
Salvation is totally and absolutely 100% dependent
upon faith in the living Word of God, Jesus Christ, and
has nothing whatsoever to do with works, either to
BE saved or to KEEP saved. Paul, in Second Timothy

writes that God "hath saved us, and called us with an holy calling, NOT ACCORDING TO OUR WORKS, but according to HIS OWN PURPOSE AND GRACE, which was given us in Christ Jesus before the world began." (II Timothy 1:9)

Salvation in the "present tense," then, has to do with the continuing work of Christ in and for us which He began in eternity past according to His absolute foreknowledge with an immutable decree. It is with this continuing "process" of deliverance from sin that the apostle is dealing when he writes:

> "But we all, with open face
> beholding as in a glass the glory of the Lord.,
> are changed into the same image
> from glory to glory,
> even as by the Spirit of the Lord."
> II Corinthians 3:18

Our experience of salvation is that of gradual change, "from glory to glory," as the Holy Spirit continues to bring the deliverance from sin which is the will of the Father and the Son for us.

"SANTIFICATION" IS NOT SIN-LESS-NESS

Although we will take up the doctrine of sanctification in connection with the study of the key Bible words "saint" and "holy," nevertheless we need to say a few things about the matter of Scriptural sanctification as it pertains directly to the doctrine of salvation in the present tense.

Sanctification is the work of the Holy Spirit in the

individual Believer, setting him apart unto the Lord
with power. As this process takes place in the day by
day experience of the born-again Christian the "old
things gradually fade away, and all things become
new." (II Corinthians 5:17) It is a process which
begins the moment we believe and continues until
that point in time when we are delivered from this
sinful nature which is so much a part of our present
bodies. It is the recognition of this fact that causes
John, the Beloved Disciple, to write:

> "If we say that we have not sinned,
> we make Him a liar,
> and His Word (Jesus Christ)
> is not in us." (I John 1:10)

I trust you have observed that in our quota-
tions of I John 1:8 (see page 82) and I John 1:10,
given above, we have put our Lord's dear name
directly alongside of the title "The Truth" (verses 8)
and of "The Word" (verse 10). As the context will
show upon examination "The Truth" and "The Word"
are titles for the Lord Jesus Christ. (Cf. also John 1:1,
and 1:14 with 14:6. This makes all claims to being
"sinless" in this life all the more blasphemous, when
one realizes that John is saying that Jesus Christ does
not dwell in the heart of the man who says that he has
not or does not sin. The "deceiver" and "father of all
lies" is Satan. To say, therefore, that one has not
sinned, or that he does not have any sin present in
his life, is to be deceived by the Deceiver and to join
him in calling God a liar. (Genesis 3:4)

GOD, AND GOD ALONE, CAN SAVE

We have already seen, in our study of the word "LORD," Jesus Christ is God manifest in the flesh, If He were anything less than Jehovah in terms of His True Being or Spirit, He could not possibly "save" us from our sins. For example the Psalmist declares:
"Salvation belongeth unto Jehovah!"
Not only is it true that only God can forgive sins, but it is also a fact that God alone can save men from their sins. Jesus Christ is Emmanuel, "God with us." If He is not True God then He cannot be Saviour! We rejoice in the constant testimony of the Scriptures as to the Deity of Christ, for all of His mighty works stand or fall as to Who He truly is as a Person.

SALVATION IN THE "FUTURE" TENSE

The future tense of the doctrine of salvation deals with the fact that we who are yet resident in the flesh shall one day be saved even from the PRESENCE of sin. This will take place when we are presented with our resurrection bodies, in which will be no sin nature whatsoever, when the Church is caught up to be with the Lord in glory forevermore. (I Thess. 1:9-10 and I Corinthians 15:51f.)

The blessed hope of the Believer is that when the Lord Jesus shall appear to catch His Bride away he (the Believer) shall be like the Saviour, without a sin nature. John indicates this with the words:
"Beloved, we are now the sons of God.
It does not yet appear what we shall be,

but we know that when He shall appear
we shall be like Him; for we shall see
Him as He is!"   (I John 3:1-3)

You and I may not finish the jobs that we start, but
the Eternal God who determined to save the Elect before He ever created a single thing always completes
everything He begins. His knowledge of the end from
the beginning keeps Him from starting something He
might not wish to finish, and His omipotence enables
Him to finish anything He may wish to start. This is
why Paul says with great assurance in Philippians 1:6:

"He who has begun a good work in you
will perform it until the Day of Jesus
Christ."

Are you BEING saved from the rule of sin? Hear
the words of Paul. "It is high time to awake out of
sleep, for now is our salvation nearer than when we
first believed!" (Romans 13:11)